Digital Transformation and Public Policies

Series Editor
Jean-Charles Pomerol

Digital Transformation and Public Policies

Current Issues

Edited by

Valérie Revest
Isabelle Liotard

WILEY

First published 2023 in Great Britain and the United States by ISTE Ltd and John Wiley & Sons, Inc.

ISTE Ltd
27-37 St George's Road
London SW19 4EU
UK

www.iste.co.uk

John Wiley & Sons, Inc.
111 River Street
Hoboken, NJ 07030
USA

www.wiley.com

Library of Congress Control Number: 2023930948

British Library Cataloguing-in-Publication Data
A CIP record for this book is available from the British Library
ISBN 978-1-78630-794-1

Contents

**Chapter 4. How to Characterize Public Innovation Platforms?
Crossed Perspectives**   111
Isabelle Liotard, Valérie Revest and Claudine Gay

Conclusion   147
Paul Cotton, Isabelle Liotard and Valérie Revest

List of Authors   161

Index   163

Acknowledgments

This collective work is the result of the Ounap (*Outils numériques et action publique*[1]) research program supported by MSH-LSE between 2018 and 2021. The research that led to the writing of Chapters 1 and 4 was also supported by the European Union's Horizon 2020 research and innovation program under grant agreement no. 822781 GROWINPRO – Growth Welfare Innovation Productivity.

We would like to thank the staff of the MSH-LSE and its director, Gilles Pollet, for their support throughout the program. We would also like to thank Carole Boulai for her support during the research project, Anne Deshors for her support during the finalization stage, as well as Lisa Hamour and Camille Barailla, students in the master's degree program in economics and social sciences at the Université Lumière Lyon 2, for their participation in this research during their master's internship. We would also like to thank the members of the Ounap research group who did not participate directly in this work, but who contributed to our thinking thanks to the exchanges that took place during many months. Our warm thanks are addressed to Philippe Barbet for his attentive re-reading of one of the chapters. His suggestions and comments were invaluable.

Chapter 4 has a special status because it is the product of many discussions and interactions with our colleagues in engineering and information sciences. It owes its existence to Aicha Sekhari and Jannik

---

1 Literally translated as Digital Tools and Public Action.

Laval of the DISP laboratory (Université Lumière Lyon 2), whom we sincerely thank for having broadened our horizon on these disciplines, and enlightening us on the possibilities of bringing the social sciences and engineering sciences together.

About the Authors

Franck Bessis is a lecturer in economics at the Université Lumière Lyon 2 and a member of the Triangle laboratory (UMR 5206). Inspired by the socio-economics of conventions, his research questions the interventions of economic knowledge in the elaboration of public policies, and in particular the uses of static microsimulation for the elaboration of socio-fiscal reforms. He has published on these themes in *Socio-économie du travail* (2017) and *Politix* (2021).

Paul Cotton is pursuing a PhD in political science (Cifre contract) under the supervision of Gilles Pollet at Sciences Po Lyon, and is attached to the Triangle laboratory (UMR 5206). His work focuses on the evolution of knowledge and repertoires of reform mobilized to transform public action at central and regional levels since 2008. In particular, he is interested in the evolution of the uses, conditions of development and factors of abandonment of public policy evaluation. He has published on the theme of economic expertise in *Politix* (2021).

Claudine Gay is a lecturer at the Université Lumière Lyon 2, deputy director of the IUT Lumière and researcher at the Triangle laboratory (UMR 5206). She is jointly responsible for the master's degree in innovation and intellectual property management and has been working on innovation for the past 20 years in a multidisciplinary approach, combining economics to understand the challenges and environment of innovation and management to understand the strategic steering and managerial aspects of innovation.

Isabelle Liotard is a lecturer in economics at the Université Sorbonne Paris Nord and a researcher at the CEPN (UMR 7234). Her research focuses on the digital economy, digital platforms and open innovation. Her work focuses on the effects of digital transformation on companies and the public sector. One field of research is the emergence of alternative organizational forms such as fablabs. She has published on these themes in the journals *Technological Forescasting and Social Change* and *Innovations*.

Valérie Revest is a professor of economics at the Université Jean Moulin Lyon 3, iaelyon School of Management, Magellan. Her research focuses on the financing of innovation, innovation platforms and the transformation of public innovation policies. She has published in international journals such as the *Journal of Evolutionary Economics* or *Industrial and Corporate Change*. She has participated in several European research projects, and was responsible for a program on digitalization and public policy.

Audrey Vézian is a research fellow in sociology and political science at the CNRS in the Triangle laboratory (UMR 5206). Her research focuses on the definition and implementation of biomedical policies as well as on their implications within the medical community. In particular, she is interested in the development of artificial intelligence in the health sector, and its consequences on the organization and practices of healthcare professionals.

Introduction

Analyzing the impact of digital transformations on public policies: a necessity

Currently, according to a broad consensus, digital technologies are radically restructuring entire industries. The multiplication and availability of vast sets of digital data from heterogeneous sources, coupled with an increasingly rapid and less costly analysis capacity, are opening the way to new expertise in fields as varied as biomedicine, mobility policies, commercial operations and even romantic relationships. This increased digitalization brought about by the growing computerization of organizations, or the development of mobile applications, connected objects, social media and collaborative platforms, is leading to profound changes in the behavior and strategies of companies. In the private sector, these technologies are driving new business models and new modes of organization and interaction, which can even take the form of hubs (Lansati and Lhakani 2017). At the global level, the most profitable companies are based on digital platforms, where a few players share markets, and expand through network effects (Evans and Schmalensee 2017). The largest capitalizations are represented by the platforms Apple, Microsoft, Alphabet and Amazon (Cusumano et al. 2019).

In line with this trend, governments also see support for the production and use of digital data as one of the pillars of their economic and social development, as demonstrated by the massive investments made in recent years in sectors as varied as health and homeland security. Of course, the

Introduction written by Isabelle LIOTARD, Valérie REVEST and Audrey VÉZIAN.

desire to translate social reality into figures to use them as a basis for government techniques is not new (Desrosières 1993). But the exponential development of digital data tends to extend and multiply the capacities of putting society into figures (Cardon 2019), and by doing so, reform the possibilities of government. Not only do all aspects of social life seem to be affected by the rise of these technologies, allowing some to foresee the possibility of identifying the laws of the social world's function (Ollion and Boelaert 2015), but also the very foundations of state architecture are being profoundly disrupted (Colin and Verdier 2015).

Indeed, the promoters of the digital revolution see in the emergence of a "new" data policy a transformation of the traditional conception of the State and its modes of intervention. The deployment of this "new form of public action" based on regulation by data (Chevallier and Cluzel-Métayer 2018) would give rise to profound recompositions in existing modes of governance. This is how new concepts – e-government, open government or citizen sourcing (Linders 2012; Nam 2012; Strasser et al. 2018) – emerge. The latter allow for the arrival of new actors, the emergence of new, more depoliticized knowledge and instruments targeting individual conduct, as well as new forms of collective action (Le Galès 2019). Deployed in a context marked by a strong mistrust of traditional political power, these digital technologies are presented as a means of addressing the democratic deficit of contemporary societies, thus feeding in a double movement the notions of open government and citizen sourcing (Nam 2012). In other words, these new technologies of government are seen by policymakers as new sources of rationality (giving an original reading of social interactions and attitudes) that are likely to contribute to an improvement of the function of political, administrative and social institutions. By simultaneously reinforcing the capacities of expression and communication as well as the possibilities of action for each individual around new collective forms (platforms, etc.) (Cardon 2019), the rise of the digital tool leads to a renewal with a form of *policy science*, "a science of public action and for public action" concerned with "improving the effectiveness of public policies by rationalizing state action" (Hassenteufel 2011). In this way, it contributes to making the knowledge generated inseparable from normative orientations, according to which, among other things, citizens would like to be not only users, but also active participants in public policy. It is in this context that new concrete modalities of public policy have emerged in the form of *smarter procurements*, new financing mechanisms, digital platforms and advanced models of public policy.

While the impact of digital technologies in the private sector is the subject of an abundant literature ((Barlatier 2016; Škare and Soriano 2021) among others), we finally know little about the variety of effects of digital technologies on the public sector, and more precisely on public policies. In the wake of the previous reflections, the purpose of this book is to study the impact of the development of digital tools on public action. The aim is to provide answers to the following questions: how does the introduction of digital technologies transform the ways in which public policies are formulated and implemented? What uses are made of these technologies, do they contribute to modifying the practices, representations and objectives of the actors involved in the conduct of public action? Finally, to what extent do digital technologies modify the relationship between the governors and the governed? More precisely, we need to consider the place and role of usage, the question of data governance and the possibility for citizens to co-construct policies with the public actor (Mergel et al. 2019).

This collective work is the result of a research program supported by the MSH-LSE between 2018 and 2021[1], and is based on an interdisciplinary approach, bringing together several HSS (Humanities and Social Science) disciplines. The use of several approaches allows for a better understanding of the issues and consequences of digitalization on public actions and policies. The dialogue within the disciplinary fields of HSS seems unavoidable to grasp an issue as complex and multidimensional as the transformation of public policies. Indeed, while political science seems to be at the heart of this issue, sociological, economic and managerial approaches are complementary to understand the different facets of the design, implementation and evaluation of public policies. Thus, this book is presented as a desire to federate complementary knowledge and skills, to set the first milestones, in order to co-construct a multidimensional approach to the issue of the impact of digital tools on public action.

New forms of governance and their effects

Following the example of many works in HSS (Cardon 2019; Mabi 2021), our approach consists of analyzing in a more precise way the

1 We would like to thank the staff of the MSH-LSE and its director, Gilles Pollet, for their support throughout the program. We would also like to sincerely thank the members of the Ounap research group who did not participate directly in this work, but who contributed to our reflection thanks to the exchanges carried out over many months.

real implications of the support policies brought to the new digital technologies in the field of public action, and more globally, in questioning the real dynamics on democratic life. However, despite the numerous obstacles identified (technical, etc.) that invite us to qualify the revolutionary dimension generated by the rise of new digital technologies (Parasie 2013; Cardon 2019), the fact remains that they structure public programs whose implementation shakes up the practices of actors (administrative, citizens, etc.) and, more globally, the daily life of the administrations in which they are implemented. The advent of the Internet at the turn of the century amplified academic studies on the subject, but at the same time increased the number of terms used to describe governments' digital transformations and their ability to foster forms of collaboration with stakeholders (Linders 2012): crowdsourcing, citizen sourcing (Torres 2007), collaborative government, Wiki Government, open government, do-it-yourself government (Dunleavy and Margetts 2010), government as a platform. In the following, we propose a preliminary terminological approach to the concepts used in this work.

From e-government to open government

The encounter between new technologies and public action has manifested itself in the concept of e-government. The latter refers to the use of information and communication technologies by public sector organizations (Janssen and Estevez 2013). The appearance of this concept in the academic literature dates back to the 1970s (Grönlund and Horan 2005). Estonia is often associated with an example of a country with a form of e-government: secure electronic identity card, centralization of individual data regarding income tax, digitalized medical prescriptions, to which are added other targeted services (Margetts and Naumann 2017). Initially, the concept of e-government focused on the provision of services to citizens and the internal workings of government. Over time, practitioners and researchers have moved away from an overly technocentric approach to focus more on the role of citizens in creating new services. According to Janssen and Estevez (2013), the concept of e-government has gone through three phases over time: the initial e-government phase (adopting ICT to deliver services), the t-government phase (transformational government: reforming the bureaucracy) and the l-government phase (lean government: doing more with less).

The notion of e-government has gradually evolved to give rise in particular to the concept of open government. In the United States, open government was one of the Obama administration's flagship projects, with the implementation of new portals giving access to new information and inviting citizens to contribute (Mergel 2015; Robert 2018). Open government is a movement particularly driven by the New Public Management (NPM) movement (Bezes 2007). On the one hand, the production of and access to massive data by public decision-makers would enable the improvement of the effectiveness of public policies, as well as democracy (Noveck 2009; Lathrop and Ruma 2010). These technologies would offer the possibility for actors to make quick decisions and solve problems in a much more flexible way (Barlatier 2016). They would thus improve the efficiency of decision-making. On the other hand, the effects of digital tools on public action would be more complex to analyze and ambivalent.

The case of Open Data is particularly revealing. This term refers to data that anyone can access, use or share. The essential criteria of Open Data are availability, reuse and distribution, and universal participation (definition of the Open Knowledge Foundation in 2005). This movement questions the limits set by various professional secrets such as statistical secrecy or tax secrecy. The tension between Open Data and professional secrecy invites us to think of certain data, in particular personal data, as "contested" public resources, in the sense that their manipulation to inform public action raises moral controversies and thus requires adjustments likely to appease the contestation[2]. What improvements are needed today to guarantee the acceptability of greater circulation of personal data within and outside the administration?

Conversely, there is also a growing reliance by the State on databases owned by private firms: examples include the use of cell phone data to measure the distribution of the population over the territory in times of containment (Semecurbe et al. 2020) or the use of cash register data to reduce the maintenance costs of the consumer price index (Blanchet and Givord 2017). In this last example, private intermediaries "contribute fully to the definition of the quality conventions of the products (goods and services)

---

2 Such a reading involves redeploying on public action the framework of analysis of "contested markets" (Steiner and Trespeuch 2014) already applied to personal data (Barraud de Lagerie and Kessous 2014).

that go into the composition of prices" (Jany-Catrice 2019, p. 38). If Open Data concerns exclusively data collected by the State, then the use of private databases to guide its action risks limiting with these new "black boxes" the promises of transparency of public action that accompany this movement. As in the case of the use of personal data for commercial purposes, this situation may give rise to new claims and lead to new arrangements regarding the ownership of this data[3].

Yu and Robinson (2012) caution about the non-interchangeability between the notions of open government and Open Data. In other words, the positive technological discussions should not hide the need for in-depth exchanges on priorities in terms of policy decisions. Moreover, the choice of data made available by public decision-makers is the result of a social construction. We select the data that we will make accessible, and that in some way reflect and correspond to the worldviews of those who want to mobilize them (Parasie 2013). These data can also be sought after by interest groups, such as lobbyists (Robert 2017), or monetized and commercialized and thus diverted from their initial objectives.

The concepts of e-government or open government cannot be understood and analyzed without comparing them with the place of stakeholders and in particular the citizen in the system. In our opinion, the term citizen must be taken in a broad definition that includes not only the average individual but also organizations from civil society (associations, NGOs, etc.), private actors (companies), researchers, etc. Citizen sourcing is a major pillar that we will define below.

From open government to citizen sourcing

The willingness of the public sector to implement citizen sourcing is a strong marker of recent years (Breul 2010; Nam 2012). The citizen can contribute to certain actions, co-produce a service jointly with the public actor and play either an active or passive role in the scheme (Androtsoupolou 2017). In this sense, they can alternately have a role of user and chooser or maker and shaper in the decisions (Lukensmeyer and Torres 2008).

---

3 In the case of mobile data, a partnership has been established between INSEE, Orange Labs and CNRS laboratories to produce a "reliable and open source method of present population and mobility statistics by combining digital and traditional data" (Semecurbe et al. 2020).

Work in public management especially sheds useful light on the devices government agencies put in place to invite citizens to help (Surowieki 2004; Lukensmeyer and Torres 2008; Misuraca 2009; Johannessen and Olsen 2010; Steen et al. 2016; Bekkers and Tummers 2018). These forms are identified under the term co-production (Bovaird and Lofler 2012) and include co-initiation, co-design, co-implementation, co-delivery and co-evaluation (Mergel 2020). Co-initation identifies needs, expected outcomes and users (Sorensen and Torfing 2018). Co-design helps improve processes to achieve desired outcomes (Nabatchi et al. 2017; Loeffler and Bovaird 2019): by incorporating user and community experience in creating, planning, improving public services, the government is part of an outside-in approach. Co-delivery occurs when outside organizations produce services with the State (Brandsen and Pestoff 2006; Brandsen and Honingh 2016) (IT service providers, user testing by users). Brandsen and Pestoff (2006) define co-delivery as:

> Co-delivery refers to a mode of organization in which citizens participate in the production of services from which they benefit, at least in part. The term can also refer to the autonomous provision of public services by citizens, without direct state intervention but with state financial support and regulatory oversight.

Finally, co-evaluation focuses on the monitoring and evaluation of public services. Traditionally, outcome evaluation activities have been carried out by public officials or external consultants. However, in the context of co-production, the State and ordinary citizens can cooperate to assess the quality of services, the problems encountered and/or the points for improvement. The co-evaluation is generally retrospective in nature; it looks to the past and is interested in activities that have already taken place. However, the results of co-evaluation exercises can be used prospectively to redesign or improve services (Nabatchi et al. 2017).

Some of the data of the administrations is the basis of their assertions in terms of public policy evaluation. Under these conditions, making these data available helps to challenge the monopoly of economic expertise historically held by the administration in France. The use by Parliament of researchers authorized to work on administrative data can also increase the proposition and evaluation capacities of the legislative branch. Within the administration itself, the circulation of data, reinforced by the Open Data movement, modifies relations between departments, by questioning the effectiveness of existing partitions. This is particularly visible when different teams within the administration work independently on the development of tools with identical purposes. The effects of Open Data can then be reinforced by those of Open Access: beyond making data available, the opening of computer codes, calculation formulas, models, algorithms, proof and government tools makes possible not only innovative controls and solutions that come from outside the State, but also simplified collaborations between its services.

The involvement of citizens (and more broadly of what we call stakeholders) in a co-construction approach with the public actor has been the subject of other works highlighting the use of digital tools to promote this imbrication. The digital environment makes it possible to set up citizen-centered governance, including in particular active citizen sourcing (Linders 2012; Mergel 2015). Knowledge sharing then becomes essential for the public actor who must set up new digital spaces that enable creativity and collaboration (Godenhjelm et al. 2018).

Linders (2012) categorizes three possible forms of connecting citizens with government via digital tools, taking three possible directions: bottom-up, top-down and transversal. The first category is based on citizen sourcing (citizen to government), whereby the citizen takes on the role of partner with the government. The public helps government to be more responsive and effective. The government holds principal responsibility, but citizens influence direction and outcomes, improve government situational awareness and can even help to execute government services on a daily basis. Linders (2012) also highlights the government as a platform (government to citizen) category: here, the government makes its knowledge and IT infrastructure available to the public who has paid for their development. By doing so, the government can help citizens improve their productivity, decision-making and daily well-being. The government is not responsible for the resulting activity, but it can leverage its platform and influence to foster greater public value. Finally, in do-it-yourself government (citizen to citizen), connected citizens can effectively self-organize and new opportunities for co-production citizen to citizen can emerge. In this informal arrangement, the government does not play an active role in the daily activities but can provide a facilitating framework. Moreover, these connections occur at three fundamental stages according to Linders (2012): at the design stage, government/citizen relations allow for reflection on the form, objectives and rules that the service will take; at the execution stage, it is about producing the public service. At the monitoring and evaluation stage, it is a matter of evaluating and possibly correcting the public service. The intersection of these three stages with the three forms of relationship leads Linders (2012) to propose Table I.1, specifying the different tools mobilized.

	Citizen sourcing	Government platform	Do-it-yourself government
Design	Consultation, sharing of ideas and opinions	Inform and influence	Self-organization of citizens
Execution/ production	Crowdsourcing and co-delivery	Ecosystem and embedding of communities of citizens	Self-service (the citizen takes care of the service)
Monitoring/evaluation	Citizen reporting activities (information, intelligence)	"Open book" government	Self-check

Table I.1. *Citizen/government relations (adapted from Linders 2012)*

General methodology and presentation of chapters

As we mentioned earlier, the ambition of our work is to grasp the real effects – desired or unexpected – of the use of digital technologies in the development of new forms of public action and/or the processes by which these effects are generated. Thus, we wish to highlight not only the characteristics of the instruments used, but also the weight of the environment and the actors' strategies in the observed dynamics in order to better question the conditions of its deployment (Kuhlman et al. 2019). This posture thus consists of being just as attentive to the consequences of public action as to the way in which they occur (Revillard 2018). Thus, we distance ourselves from purely evaluative and/or forecasting research insofar as the question of the effectiveness of public action cannot be limited to an analysis of the compliance (or non-compliance) of the targeted results. Therefore, by giving different disciplinary approaches – economic sciences, political sciences and sociology – it is more broadly an issue of questioning (putting into discussion) how the rise of digital technology in society invites us to reinvent our modes of knowledge production and evaluation of public action.

This book is organized into four chapters. Chapter 1 examines the impact of digitalization on the European Commission's (EC) innovation policy through the mobilization of new political instruments: platform-based innovation contests. According to the authors, I. Liotard and V. Revest, this innovation incentive scheme is a first response to the EC's desire to implement a policy of stimulating and supporting open and inclusive innovation, following both the model advocated by Chesbrough (2006) in the private sector and the orientation given by the concept of responsible research and innovation developed by Europe. The results tend to show that if the contest system reveals a certain degree of openness compared to more traditional policy instruments, they could tend towards more inclusiveness of citizens in the different phases of the competition. In addition, a lack of multidisciplinarity is observed among the mobilized stakeholders. This research thus illustrates the attempts of a public decision-maker to transform its mode of action by using a device derived from crowdsourcing. This research is based on the exploitation of official documents, on the EC web portal, as well as on interviews conducted with competition managers.

The issue of access to health data is at the heart of Chapter 2. Indeed, from the 1990s, the latter aroused great enthusiasm on the part of public and private actors under the joint impetus of the explosion of data production in this field and the increase in computing power capacities at lower cost, facilitating their linking. The author, A. Vézian, highlights, on the one hand, the beneficial effects of this abundance: facilitating access to public health databases, stimulating research based on the application of artificial intelligence to health data, and promoting the transfer of innovations in the private sector. However, on the other hand, it points to the questions related to the mode of regulation of this data policy by examining the characteristics of the mechanisms of governance in the French health sector. The latter appear stabilized around a strong proximity between health professionals and political personnel, by the central role of alliances between State/scientists/companies, and finally by strong institutional constraints leading to a weak convergence within the health administration of the processing of Big Data applied to health. This chapter is based on the analysis of the grey literature in this field as well as on a series of interviews with the administrative and professional actors involved in these approaches.

In the context of public action, data can be used to feed theoretical models. This is the issue addressed by F. Bessis and P. Cotton in Chapter 3, through the examination of microsimulation models used to evaluate redistribution policies. The authors show the role played by microsimulation actors in this policy of data accessibility, and address the issue of maintaining a plurality and a sharing of expertise and conventions between administrations and academics. This work is based on a historical perspective of the current configuration, reconstructed from a series of interviews conducted with actors who have contributed to the development of these models and their dissemination over the past 30 years.

Chapter 4 takes the form of an original essay proposing a reflection on the notion of public platforms from an interdisciplinary approach that crosses the views of the social sciences (economics and management) and the engineering sciences. This cross-reading highlights the multiple facets of platforms oriented towards economic and managerial objectives as well as their diversity. The authors, I. Liotard, V. Revest and C. Gay, focus on platforms intended to support innovation. The two main contributions of this chapter are the following. First, a new concept is proposed: that of "public innovation intermediary platforms", based on the study of two innovation intermediation platforms (private and public). Second, engineering sciences pay particular attention to the design of this type of platform, which can be useful to the public actor in deploying these tools.

References

Androutsopoulou, A., Karacapilidis, N., Loukis, E., Chaealabidis, Y. (2017). Towards an integrated and inclusive platform for open innovation in the public sector. *E-Democracy–Privacy-Preserving, Secure, Intelligent E-Government Services: 7th International Conference, E-Democracy 2017*, Athens.

Barlatier, P.J. (2016). Management de l'innovation et nouvelle ère numérique – Enjeux et perspectives. *Revue française de gestion*, 42(254), 55–63.

Barraud de Lagerie, P. and Kessous, E. (2014). La mise en marché des "données personnelles" ou la difficile extension du marché à la personne. In *Marchés contestés : quand le marché rencontre la morale*, Steiner, P. and Trespeuch, M. (eds). Presses Universitaire du Mirail, Toulouse.

Bekkers, V. and Tummers, L. (2018). Innovation in the public sector: Towards an open and collaborative approach. *International Review of Administrative Sciences*, 84(2), 209–213.

Bezes, P. (2007). Construire des bureaucraties wébériennes à l'ère du New Public Management ? *Critique Internationale*, 2, 9–29.

Blanchet, D. and Givord, P. (2017). Données massives, statistique publique et mesure de l'économie. In L'économie française. Comptes et dossiers. Report, Institut National de la Statistique et des Études Économiques, Paris, 59–77.

Bovaird, T. and Lofler, E. (2012). From engagement to co-production: The contribution for users and communities to outcomes and public value. *Voluntas: International Journal of Voluntary and Nonprofit Organizations*, 23(4), 1119–1138.

Brandsen, T. and Honingh, M. (2016). Distinguishing different types of coproduction: A conceptual analysis based on the classical definitions. *Public Administration Review*, 76(3), 427–435.

Brandsen, T. and Pestoff, V. (2006). Co-production, the third sector and the delivery of public services: An introduction. *Public Management Review*, 8(4), 493–501.

Breul, J.D. (2010). Practitioner's perspective – Improving sourcing decisions. *Public Administration Review*, 70(s1), s193–s200.

Cardon, D. (2019). *Culture numérique*. Presses de Sciences Po, Paris.

Chevallier, J. and Cluzel-Métayer, L. (2018). Introduction. *Revue française d'administration publique*, 3(167), 463–470.

Colin, N. and Verdier, H. (2015). *L'âge de la multitude – Entreprendre et gouverner après la révolution numérique*. Dunod, Paris.

Collège d'experts (2020). Faire de la France une économie de rupture technologique. Soutenir les marchés émergents à forts enjeux de compétitivité. Report to the Ministre de l'Économie et des finances and the Ministre de l'Enseignement supérieur, de la recherche et de l'innovation, Paris.

Cusumano, M.A., Gawer, A., Yoffie, D.B. (2019). *The Business of Platforms. Strategy in the Age of Digital Competition, Innovation, and Power*. HarperCollins, New York.

Desrosières, A. (1993). *La politique des grands nombres. Histoire de la raison statistique*. La Découverte, Paris.

Evans, D.S. and Schmalensee, R. (2017). *De précieux intermédiaires : comment Blablacar, Facebook, Paypal ou Uber créent de la valeur*. Odile Jacob, Paris.

Godenhjelm, S. and Johanson J.E. (2018). Les effets de l'inclusion des parties prenantes sur l'innovation dans les projets du secteur public. *Revue internationale des sciences administratives*, 84(1), 47–67.

Grönlund, Å. and Horan, T.A. (2005). Introducing e-gov: History, definitions, and issues. *Communications of the Association for Information Systems*, 15(1), 713–729.

Hassenteufel, P. (2011). *Sociologie politique : l'action publique.* Armand Colin, Paris.

Iansiti, M. and Lakhani, K.R. (2017). Managing our hub economy. *Harvard Business Review*, 10, 117.

Janssen, M. and Estevez, E. (2013). Lean government and platform-based governance – Doing more with less. *Government Information Quarterly*, 30, S1–S8.

Jany-Catrice, F. (2019). L'indice des prix à la consommation en France : acteurs et conflits autour de sa mesure. *Revue française de socio-économie*, 22(1), 19–43.

Johannessen, J.A. and Olsen, B. (2010). The future of value creation and innovations: Aspects of a theory of value creation and innovation in a global knowledge economy. *International Journal of Information Management*, 30(6), 502–511.

Kuhlmann, S., Stegmaier, P., Konrad, K. (2019). The tentative governance of emerging science and technology – A conceptual introduction. *Research Policy*, 48(5), 1091–1097.

Lathrop, D. and Ruma, L. (2010). *Open Government: Collaboration, Transparency, and Participation in Practice.* O'Reilly Media, Newton.

Le Galès, P. (2019). Gouvernance. In *Dictionnaire des politiques*, Boussaguet, L. (ed.). Presses de Sciences, Paris.

Linders, D. (2012). From e-government to we-government: Defining a typology for citizen coproduction in the age of social media. *Government Information Quarterly*, 29(4), 446–454.

Lukensmeyer, C.J. and Torres, L.H. (2008). Citizensourcing: Citizen participation in a networked nation. In *Civic Engagement in a Network Society*, Yang, K. and Bergrud, E. (eds). Information Age Publishing, Charlotte.

Mabi, C. (2021). La "civic tech" et "la démocratie numérique" pour "ouvrir" la démocratie ? *Réseaux*, 225, 215–248.

Margetts, H. and Naumann, A. (2017). Government as a platform: What can Estonia show the world? Research document, University of Oxford.

Mergel, I. (2015). Opening government: Designing open innovation processes to collaborate with external problem solvers. *Social Science Computer Review*, 33(5), 599–612.

Mergel, I. (2020). La co-création de valeur publique par les directions du numérique : une comparaison internationale. *Action publique, recherche et pratique*, 6, 6–16.

Mergel, I., Edelmann, N., Haug, N. (2019). Defining digital transformation: Results from expert interviews. *Government Information Quarterly*, 36(4), 101385.

Misuraca, G.C. (2009). e-Government 2015: Exploring m-government scenarios, between ICT-driven experiments and citizen-centric implications. *Technology Analysis & Strategic Management*, 21(3), 407–424.

Nabatchi, T., Sancino, A., Sicilia, M. (2017). Varieties of participation in public services: The who, when, and what of co-production. *Public Administration Review*, 77(5), 766–776.

Nam, T. (2012). Suggesting frameworks of citizen-sourcing via Government 2.0. *Government Information Quarterly*, 29(1), 12–20.

Ollion, É. and Boelaert, J. (2015). Au-delà des big data. Les sciences sociales et la multiplication des données numériques. *Sociologie*, 6, 295–310 [Online]. Available at: https://doi-org.ezp.em-lyon.com/.

Parasie, S. (2013). Des machines à scandale : éléments pour une sociologie morale des bases de données. *Réseaux*, 178–179, 127–161.

Revillard, A. (2018). Saisir les conséquences d'une politique à partir de ses ressortissants : la réception de l'action publique. *Revue française de science politique*, 68, 469–491.

Robert, C. (2018). La transparence comme nouvel horizon des démocraties européennes. *Politique européenne*, 3, 8–43.

Semecurbe, F., Suarez Castillo, M., Galiana, L., Coudin, É., Poulhes, M. (2020). Que peut faire l'Insee à partir des données de téléphonie mobile ? Mesure de population présente en temps de confinement et statistiques expérimentales. *Le blog de l'Insee* [Online]. Available at: https://blog.insee.fr/que-peut-faire-linsee-a-partir-des-donnees-de-telephonie-mobile-mesure-de-population-presente-en-temps-de-confinement-et-statistiques-experimentales/ [Accessed 2 November 2021].

Škare, M. and Soriano, D.R. (2021). A dynamic panel study on digitalization and firm's agility: What drives agility in advanced economies 2009–2018. *Technological Forecasting and Social Change*, 163, 120418.

Sørensen, E. and Torfing, J. (2018). Co-initiation of collaborative innovation in urban spaces. *Urban Affairs Review*, 54(2), 388–418.

Steen, T., Nabatchi, T., Brand, D. (2016). Introduction: Special issue on the coproduction of public services. *International Review of Administrative Sciences*, 82(1), 3–7.

Steiner, P. and Trespeuch, M. (2014). *Marchés contestés : quand le marché rencontre la morale*. Presses Universitaire du Mirail, Toulouse.

Strasser, B., Baudry, J., Mahr, D., Sanchez, G., Tancoigne, E. (2019). "Citizen science"? Rethinking science and public participation. *Science & Technology Studies*, 32(2), 52–76.

Surowiecki, J. (2004). *The Wisdom of Crowds: Why the Many Are Smarter Than the Few and How Collective Wisdom Shapes Business, Economies, Societies and Nations*. Random House, New York.

Torres, L.H. (2007). Citizen sourcing in the public interest. *Knowledge Management for Development Journal*, 3(1), 134–145.

Yu, H. and Robinson, D.G. (2012). The new ambiguity of open government. *UCLA Law Review Discourse*, 59(178), 180–208.

From Crowdsourcing to Inclusiveness: The European Experience of Innovation Contests

For about a decade, the European Commission (EC) and the governments involved have been engaged in transforming their modes of action towards more transparency, interoperability and citizen satisfaction (European Commission 2013; Mergel and Haug 2019). This desire for metamorphosis is intrinsically linked to the deployment of new technologies. Indeed, the digital transition in the public sector is introducing new ways of working and interacting with stakeholders. The design and implementation of all public policies are affected, and this is particularly the case for policies supporting research and innovation at the European level. In 2016, the European Commissioner for Research, Innovation and Science, Carlos Moedas, published a report entitled "Open innovation – Open science". This report defines the principles of the concept of open innovation (OI) exposing the main directions for the future. First, the OI movement must rely on crowdsourcing (calling on the expertise or ideas of the crowd) to stimulate the development of a broad innovative ecosystem (Guittard and Schenk 2016; Renault 2017). Second, it must be inclusive: "integrating stakeholders and including citizens into innovative processes". The innovation contests linked to the EC's digital portal and launched during the Commission's Horizon 2020 program are part of this dynamic (see the report: Open innovation, open science, open to the world. A vision for Europe 2016). An

Chapter written by Isabelle LIOTARD and Valérie REVEST.

innovation contest is commonly defined as a challenge launched and financed by a sponsor (private and/or public), dealing with various issues (technological, societal, environmental), and for which the winner(s) receive a monetary or non-monetary prize (Scotchmer 2006).

Five years after the publication of the Moedas' report, the objective of this chapter is to understand the way in which the EC, through the innovation contests, is engaged in an open innovation movement. In particular, the aim is to analyze how a crowdsourcing practice including a dimension of inclusiveness can be implemented. To what extent have the recommendations of the 2016 report been followed?

In order to answer this question, we propose studying the functioning of two European innovation contests – *Blockchain for Social Good* and *Affordable High-Tech for Humanitarian Aid-*, focusing on their ability to integrate the engagement of various stakeholders during the various stages of the competition. Previous research conducted on the first contests initiated by the EC was rather critical: the mobilization of the contests was not yet in line with the 2016 recommendations (Liotard and Revest 2021). Here, we show progress in terms of openness, collaboration and inclusiveness. However, a real approach including the active contribution of stakeholders during the different stages of the competition is still far from being perfectly accomplished. From a methodological point of view, we rely on a review of official site documents, as well as on interviews with contest managers from the European Commission. From an academic point of view, the chapter contributes to a reflection on the question of the co-production of knowledge within innovation processes between the public sector and other actors (individual or collective representing the private, public, academic or associative sector).

In the first section, we review the concepts of open innovation (OI) and crowdsourcing, first deployed in the private sector and then in the public sector. The second section is devoted to the presentation of innovation contests based on public digital platforms. The third section is dedicated to the study of two contests launched by the European Commission in the context of the European Innovation Council (EIC). Future avenues for improving the action of public actors in the mobilization of contests are presented in the fourth section.

1.1. Open innovation and crowdsourcing: two closely related phenomena

Numerous publications in economics and management over the past two decades have highlighted the phenomenon of open innovation (OI): the work of Chesbrough (2003, 2006) and Von Hippel (2005) has helped to understand this new way of innovating[1], driven by digital technology and the Internet, in a context where the need to innovate more quickly and at lower cost has become essential. This paradigm leads private actors to set up outside-in and inside-out innovation mechanisms, and to couple them if necessary (Gassman and Enkel 2004). Through outside-in, the company uses all means to capture knowledge (licenses, partnerships, innovations, co-construction with users, with suppliers, even with competitors, etc.), and through inside-out, its objective is to give value to its own knowledge (licenses, spin-offs, industrial partnerships, etc.). The challenge is simple: to extend the firm's borders to enable it to seek knowledge from outside in order to enrich its own internal knowledge, and to do so by calling on a diversity of actors, both those who are part of its network and those who are completely new.

The OI mechanism carried by the Internet, thanks to the possibilities offered by digital technology, takes on another facet that Jullien and Pénin (2014) will call OI 2.0. The company calls upon new individuals and/or new organizations (outside-in), potentially vectors of new and creative solutions, via crowdsourcing. This process, the term for which was coined by Howes in 2006, is most often considered as a means of deploying OI and has been the subject of abundant literature since this date. Part of the outside-in movement of OI and driven by the advent of digital networks, it allows an organization to call upon the expertise of members of a crowd (Burger-Helmchen and Pénin 2011; Guittard and Schenk 2011). This approach is in line with the desire to attract individuals already present on Web 2.0 so that they can participate in the creation of value for these companies. By contributing specific knowledge and answering questions, Internet users (regardless of their profile) constitute an immense reservoir of knowledge that companies can use to develop and quickly market products.

---

1 The concept of open innovation was popularized by Chesbrough and presented as a new way of innovating, but for some researchers, a form of open innovation was already present in some previous innovative processes. See, for example, the critique by Isckia and Lescop (2011).

The cases of P&G (Huston and Sakkab 2006) and Lego (Taspscott and Williams 2007) are illuminating from this point of view. The phenomenon of crowdsourcing is very often associated with individual problem solving, in which individuals do not cooperate with each other (Lebraty and Lobre 2010; Pénin et al. 2013). A widely adopted definition of this concept is offered by Estellés-Arolas and González-Ladrón-De-Guevara (2012), based on a literature review and the main commonalities of various forms of crowdsourcing:

> Crowdsourcing is a type of online participatory activity in which an individual, an institution, a non-profit organization or a company proposes to a group of individuals of varying knowledge, heterogeneity and number, via a flexible open call, to voluntarily undertake a task. The realization of the task, of variable complexity and modularity, in which the crowd must participate by contributing their labor, money, knowledge and/or experience, always implies a mutual benefit. The user will receive satisfaction of a given type of need, be it economic, social recognition, self-esteem, or individual skill development, while the crowdsourcer will obtain and use to its advantage what the user has contributed to the company, the form of which will depend on the type of activity undertaken (Estellés-Arolas and González-Ladrón-De-Guevara 2012, p. 197).

In parallel, and on the basis of this characterization, several typologies of crowdsourcing have been constructed in order to capture the different dimensions of crowdsourcing (Brabham 2009; Burger-Helmchen and Pénin 2011; Guittard and Schenk 2011; Pénin et al. 2013) (Table 1.1). These typologies generally highlight three main dimensions: the type of resources/skills that the crowd can contribute (Howe 2008), the type of tasks offered to the crowd (Lebraty and Lobre-Lebraty 2013; Pénin et al. 2013; Renaud 2017) and the forms of interactions between the groups of actors involved (Pisano and Verganti 2008; Hutter et al. 2011; Renaud 2017). For example, Renaud (2017) highlights four crowdsourcing profiles related to the forms of interaction between the members of the crowd: cumulative, collaborative, competitive and cooperative crowdsourcing. For their part, Hutter et al. (2011) focus on the behaviors of users in the context of a private contest, and determine possible[2] configurations of intervention and

---

2 In the literature and in practice, the term "prizes" is also used instead of "contests".

interference, according to the degree of their contribution. Table 1.1 shows the different forms of crowdsourcing identified in the academic literature.

Forms of crowdsourcing	Characterization
Forms of interaction (Renaud 2017)	Cooperative, competitive, collaborative, cumulative
Types of resources (Howe 2008)	Collective intelligence, crowd work and creativity, crowd opinion, crowd funding
Types of tasks and assignments (Penin et al. 2013; Renaud 2017)	Simple and routine tasks, complex tasks and inventive activities, creative tasks
Types of activities offered (Lebraty and Lobre-Lebraty 2013)	Crowdjobbing, crowdwisdom, crowdfunding, forecasting, innovation, authenticity, crowd auditing, crowdcontrol, crowdcuration, crowdcare
Types of users (Hutter et al. 2011)	The competitors, the cooperators, the communicators, the observers

Table 1.1. *The main types of crowdsourcing in the literature of economics and management sciences*

1.2. Platforms, innovation contests and inclusiveness or how to better articulate innovation and society?

In the case of OI with crowdsourcing, the search for expertise can be based on sites set up by the companies themselves (Orange, Google, Microsoft, Siemens, etc.) with a direct appeal to the crowd. Another alternative is the use of digital platforms that implement an innovation contest. The latter is commonly defined as a challenge launched and financed by a sponsor (private or public), dealing with various issues (technological, societal, environmental), and for which the winner(s) receives a monetary or non-monetary prize (Scotchmer 2006). In reality, the innovation contest is a very old mechanism for stimulating innovation that is part of the development history of the major industrialized countries (Adler 2011). These contests generally focus on different rents: the search for advice, an idea, the competing of Internet users to create a logo or even a more complex request around innovative challenges (Liotard and Revest 2018). The advent of the Internet and digitalization have provided a new medium for this incentive mechanism, as contests are now backed by platforms and use crowdsourcing. Thus, digital platforms with contests bring together an organization with a request for innovation (advice, idea or more complex request) and the Internet users as a whole. The idea is to stimulate innovation in the predefined and desired directions. While the first innovation intermediation platforms were the responsibility of the private sector (Innocentive, NineSigma, etc. (Lakhani and Panetta 2007; Liotard and Revest 2018)), they represent one of the new tools recently mobilized by public actors in the field of innovation policies.

However, their adoption as policy instruments to encourage innovation is not self-evident. The first "public" users of this type of device were U.S. federal agencies. In 2009, the administration of U.S. President Barak Obama published a report marking a turning point in U.S. innovation strategy ("A strategy for American Innovation: driving towards sustainable growth and quality jobs")[3].

Among the avenues explored, that of innovation contests has been clearly expressed through the creation of *Grand Challenges*, major societal challenges proposed by the American public administration. For example, with regard to climate change, *The Climate Change in Focus* was launched by the US Environmental Protection Agency, aimed at students, with the objective of producing a video to raise awareness of the effects of climate change. The impulsion of the 2009 US New Innovation Strategy document has since led to an acceleration in the use of contests by American public authorities, whether through the creation of a website or the publication of laws[4]. The "Guidance on the Use of Challenges and Prizes to Promote Open Government" (2010) provided practical guidance on the procedure to follow, and gave a whole series of recommendations to the American federal agencies on how to choose the appropriate type of contest, on the form of awards to be granted, on the question of intellectual property, etc. With regard to encouraging innovation, the agencies were used to mobilize traditional instruments such as subsidies, or public tender mechanisms: they

---

3 http://www.innovationamerica.us/images/stories/pdf/sept20innovationwhitepaper_final.pdf.

4 In 2006, legislation was passed in Congress to allow the NSF (National Science Foundation) to establish a bounty program to stimulate innovation (Science, State, Justice, and Related Agencies Appropriations Act – public Law, 109–108) (Brennan et al. 2011). In the same year, Congress passed the H Prize Act, which authorized the Secretary of Energy to establish a program to award prizes to promote advances in research, development and commercial applications of hydrogen energy technologies (NRC 2007). This law is related to the NASA "Authorization Act" passed in 2005, allowing the agency to offer incentives to stimulate innovation for basic or applied research, technology development or prototype demonstrations (Kalil 2006). See also America COMPETES ACT (2007).

therefore did not have the skills to implement online innovation contests. In September 2010, all these recommendations resulted in the creation of the Challenge.Gov site, allowing agencies and parastatal organizations to put their own contests online[5]. Since 2010, academic research has been conducted to analyze and assess how US federal agencies have used this new instrument (see the work of Kay (2011, 2017) and Mergel (2015, 2018) and Chapter 4).

From his doctoral dissertation, entitled "How do prizes induce innovation? Learning from the Google Lunar Prize", Luciano Kay has developed a number of managerial recommendations in terms of the use of contests, which were then taken up in the report "Managing Innovation Prizes in Government" (2011). The objective of Kay's research is to show the extent to which innovation contests represent an alternative policy instrument to traditional instruments such as grants and contracts, in order to enable US federal agencies to achieve the political objectives set. First, contests are generally considered as a complementary solution to existing systems, and not an alternative (Adler 2011). Second, their implementation, making it possible to reduce the administrative and fiscal barriers attached to standard forms of subsidies and contracts, is, however, not easy since contests are associated with more uncertainty in terms of input and output than traditional instruments. Indeed, at the time of the call to the crowd, the number and profile of solution providers are not known and the results only emerge at the end of the competition[6]. As a result, contests are not suitable for all innovation objectives and all economic policies. They appear to be more in line with challenges relating to radical and theoretical innovations (Kay 2018). Moreover, the literature emphasizes its complementary role to other forms of incentive for innovation: patents, research contracts, calls for tenders, etc. Third, the success of contests depends on a rigorous and appropriate establishment of their parameters. According to Kay (2011), public decision-makers should launch them in a targeted manner that complements other innovation support tools. More specifically, contests as instruments encouraging innovation seem to correspond more to the following situations:

---

5 So far, around $31 million has been paid out in monetary awards. More than 300 contests were submitted and nearly 42,000 participants responded (source: www.digitalgov.gov).

6 With traditional innovation incentive instruments, the carriers of solutions are in a certain way chosen (mechanisms of grants and calls for tenders), and the solutions to be achieved can be predefined in advance.

– when the research programs involve a very high level of R&D;

– when unconventional approaches are needed;

– when it is possible to draw on external resources to support the evolution of the agencies' missions.

Thus, the results of Kay's (2011) work highlight a number of steps and parameters that must be taken into account by public decision-makers wishing to mobilize this type of tool (Table 1.2).

A reflection on the effectiveness of public contests highlights the key factors that drive it: (1) focusing on appropriate contest design; (2) proposing a challenging, ambitious but feasible project; (3) initiating collaborations and partnerships; (4) trying to be inclusive and encouraging diversity; (5) promoting the contest program in the public sphere; and (6) learning from experience. In more recent research on the topic of contests, the evaluation of contests launched (Kay et al. 2017), the authors emphasize the importance of the inclusive dimension of contests. Contests must respond favorably to two questions: did the inclusive nature of the contest attract unintended applicants? Do the solutions have a socially desirable effect? Among the factors that can increase the success and effectiveness of public contests are partnerships, and the creation of diversity and inclusiveness of stakeholders.

In recent years, the notion of inclusiveness has been at the heart of public decision-makers in terms of innovation and related public policies. Whether in the United States or in Europe, the reflection undertaken for an innovation process marked by the consideration of (all) stakeholders is complementary to the desire to move towards OI. The various reports from the American (GAO 2017) or European (Horizon 2020 program) administrations bear witness to this desire. The responsible research and innovation (RRI) approach is particularly relevant for understanding the notion of inclusiveness (Gay et al. 2019). Moving towards responsible research and innovation calls for a profound institutional transformation of research and innovation processes, which has recently been taken up by the economic literature. Stilgoe et al. (2012) define RRI as integrating and developing skills of anticipation, reflexivity, inclusiveness and responsiveness. The term "inclusiveness" here refers to the concept of inclusive deliberation, described in Box 1.1 by Owen and Pansera (2019).

Steps of the contest	Actions to be taken
Develop the contest architecture with multiple stakeholders (design stage)	Define the objectives of the contest Determine the reward (type and amount) Indicate eligible participants Produce the rules of the contest Secure the financing process Identify intellectual property rights
Implement the contest with stakeholders	Seek collaborations and partnerships Communicate about the contest Manage the competition Determine the winner(s) and award the prize Use the results of the competition
Evaluate the contest (ex post) with stakeholders	Define the criteria for the evaluation

Table 1.2. *The essential steps in the development of an open contest (source: Kay (2011))*

Description: opening up the fields of possibility, visions, goals, processes and impacts of science, technology and innovation to achieve an inclusive deliberation. The latter takes the form of invitation, engagement, early and iterative deliberation with a diverse range of stakeholders and audiences in setting the research and innovation agenda. It includes knowledge and support for legitimate decision-making. Interdisciplinarity and transdisciplinarity aim at the coproduction of knowledge.

Objectives: to engage stakeholders and audiences. Stimulate debate. Understand the different framings. Identify opportunities for innovation. Make visible the assumptions, commitments and expected effects. Participation in agenda setting and societal challenges. Equitable decision-making. Better capacity and basis for sound and legitimate decision-making.

Box 1.1. *The inclusive deliberation dimension according to Owen and Pansera (2019)*

While the US contests offered by federal agencies via the dedicated website[7] have been widely studied (Desouza and Mergel 2013; Mergel 2018, see Chapter 4), little work has been done on the European contests launched during the H2020 program. The existing literature corresponds essentially to professional articles, press articles and EC institutional communication, but no in-depth academic study has been undertaken. Our work is thus in line with the research of Murray et al. (2016) and Mergel (2018) on public innovation contests in the United States using case studies. A first study of initial European contests in 2021 by the authors provided a preliminary portrait of the modes of organization of the latter (Liotard and Revest 2021). In the following section, we explore two recently launched European contests, placing them against both the criteria of public OI and inclusiveness.

1.3. The European context: a proactive approach to open innovation

The European project of stimulating innovation has a long history and has been supported since the constitution of Europe by successive treaties (Gonzalez-Fernandez et al. 2019). The different plans in favor of innovation research have been concretized by Horizon 2020 and more recently by Horizon Europe (2021–2027), the 9^e Framework Programme. Innovation in European policies occupies a major place, due to its economic, technological and societal impacts, not only within Europe but also on the international scene in relation to the main competing countries or areas. The reaffirmation of the importance of innovation for employment and growth was expressed in particular by the Lisbon Treaty (2009) and, since then, public policies have continued to implement measures to meet these challenges.

For some authors, the move towards a more dynamic innovation policy needs to be realized from a more holistic and complex conceptual framework, similar to the triple helix scheme (Etzkowitz and Leydesdorff 2000) that allows for a comprehensive understanding of the European innovation ecosystem (Gonzalez-Fernandez et al. 2019). Governments with the EC, industry and the academic world would be at the heart of a node allowing regulation, production and dissemination of knowledge for society according to Etzhowitz (2003). According to this perspective, at the

---

7 www.challenge.gov.

European level, OI appears to be a major key to nurturing these interactions. European authorities have been interested in these practices for several years, as they see them as a solution to boost European innovation policy. As early as 2012, the importance of these links was highlighted "[…] between the Digital Agenda and open innovation creating societal and structural capital for competitiveness and sustainable development"[8]. The report "Boosting open innovation and knowledge transfer in the European union" (2014) highlights actions to be implemented around open innovation and co-creation practices to install a favorable innovation ecosystem through OI 2.0, based on the networking of ecosystem actors and "multicollaborative" innovation. "Within such an ecosystem the relevant participants engage with each other, through multiple channels, even by the means of pooling their internal resources and equipment, including knowledge, technology, finance, people, markets, and data" (Boosting open innovation and knowledge transfer in the European union, p. 26). This 2014 report forms a fundamental basis for the 2016 report "Open Innovation, open science, open to the world" in which the role of OI 2.0 is reaffirmed and greatly emphasized as a means of responding to two juxtapositions: the need to put the user or citizen at the heart of the innovative device (user-centric), on the one hand, and to create an ecosystem that allows for co-creation mechanisms at all levels, on the other. The recent 2018 report anchors this need:

> Engage and involve citizens and civil society organisations in co-designing and co-creating responsible research and innovation agendas and contents, promoting science education, making scientific knowledge publicly accessible, and facilitating participation by citizens and civil society organisations in its activities[9] (European Commission 2014, p. 4).

OI within the EC is then apprehended as a concept in perpetual evolution, oriented towards the constitution of open ecosystems, characterized by collaborative innovations that are part of networks. A particular institutional dispositive, the EIC (European Innovation Council), is being set up by

---

8 *Open innovation*, EC 2012, p. 8.
9 European Commission. European Commission COM (2018). 435 Final: Proposal Establishing Horizon Europe – the Framework Programme for Research and Innovation, LaOSTg Down Its Rules for Participation and Dissemination. European Commission. Volume 0224, Brussels, Belgium, 2018.

European Commissioner Carlos Moedas in 2018 (Weber et al. 2019). The central role of the EIC is to address the weaknesses inherent in the H2020 program, foster ecosystem collaboration and stimulate European-wide research. A pilot program of EIC is proposed as of October 2017 in the Work Programme H2020 (2018–2020). It was on this occasion that contest-identified EIC prizes were launched with a global budget of 40 million euros.

1.4. European contests and inclusiveness: two case studies

In 2015, the European Commission, through its H2020 program (2014–2020), a European research and innovation program, posted its first innovation contests on its portal, complementary to other innovation support tools. These contests have been launched in various fields, both technological and societal (Makela 2017). The initiative follows other similar schemes set up at the national level in some European countries such as the UK's Nesta program. In practice, the European contests are visible on the DG Research and Innovation (DG RTD) portal[10], via the finance tab. A page is dedicated to each contest (the former Horizon Prize contests are still presented there as well as the recent contests; see Table 1.3). Although most of them are focused on complex and technological issues, some of them also address social and societal concerns[11].

The implementation of the first contests created by the European Commission from 2015 has been the subject of three main criticisms, vis-à-vis a perspective of open innovation and inclusiveness. First, the choice of subject and mode of operation of the contest depended only on the team in charge within the European Commission, with a relatively hierarchical mode of operation. Second, the stakeholders were little mobilized (associations, civil society actors, etc.) throughout the process. They only participated in the preparatory meeting before the launch of the contest, and in the final evaluation jury. Third, the stakeholders came from the same disciplinary sector as the main subject of the contest (e.g. biology, chemistry, computer science, etc.) (Liotard and Revest 2021).

---

10 https://ec.europa.eu/info/research-and-innovation_en.

11 For example, a prize launched every year rewards the best European woman who has innovated and created her start-up: EU Prize for Women Innovators. Interested candidates can consult all the information about the contest (rules, amount of the prize, deadlines, videos, additional documents, etc.) and are redirected to another page to submit their proposal.

Since then, the European Commission has continued to exploit this innovation citation system and has attempted to develop it further. Our study aims to determine whether recent contests are more open and inclusive and, if so, at what levels of the contest process. To this end, we examine the properties of their organizational architecture, i.e. the sequence of steps as well as the rules that govern the functioning of a competition. We have thus chosen to analyze the following contests: *Affordable High-Tech for Humanitarian Aid* and *Blockchain for Social Goods*, among the 22 contests launched since 2015 by the European Commission[12]. There are two main reasons for this choice: first, they are among the six contests proposed by the European Innovation Council (EIC) under the new Horizon Europe framework program (Table 1.3).

	Launch date	End date	Prize
Affordable high-tech for humanitarian aid	4th quarter 2017	1st quarter 2020	1 million euros
Fuel from the sun: artificial photosynthesis	4th quarter 2017	1st quarter 2021	5 million euros
Innovative batteries for eVehicles	February 23, 2018	December 17, 2020	10 million euros
Early warning for epidemics	April 26, 2018	September 01, 2020	5 million euros
Blockchains for social good	May 16, 2018	September 03, 2019	1 million euros
Low-cost space launch	June 12, 2018	June 01, 2021	10 million euros

Table 1.3. *Recent contests launched by the EIC (European Innovation Council)[13]*

Second, what these two contests have in common is that they address societal challenges while relying on technological innovations. In other words, they are not based solely on one discipline, but on the combination of several disciplines, combining technological challenge and response to societal needs (e.g. biology, computer science and sociology). Thus, they contribute to following the demands for openness to society, as mentioned in the Commission's reports (2014, 2016). "This means that a specific innovation can no longer be seen as the result of predefined and isolated

12 For a more global view of the 22 contests, see: http://www.growinpro.eu/open-innovation-and-prizes-is-the-european-commission-really-comitted/.
13 https://eic.ec.europa.eu/eic-funding-opportunities/eic-prizes/eic-horizon-prizes_en#ecl-inpage-252.

innovation activities but rather as the outcome of a complex co-creation process involving knowledge flows across the entire economic and social environment" (European Commission 2016).

Our demonstration is based on a narrative approach following Van Eeten (2007). Approaches based on arguments or narrations are considered to be devices that make particular sense for studying processes of a political nature (Arrona and Zabala-Iturriagagoitia 2019). Furthermore, the case study is recognized as particularly relevant in fields under construction where new conceptualizations are sought (Eisenhardt 1989). In addition, in parallel to the official documents, sites, etc., for these contests, we had the opportunity to conduct two long interviews with stakeholders involved in the organization of these involved in the organization of these contests. These interviews were recorded and transcribed.

1.4.1. *Blockchain for social goods (BCSG): a step towards greater inclusiveness?*

The contest BCSG was launched in May 2018 and the competition ended in September 2019. With a prize of €5 million split between five winners (of which there were eventually six at the end of the competition), the contest aimed to reward advanced technologies (at the TRL7 level)[14] in the field of distributed ledgers, for which blockchain is the best known illustration. The objective of the contest was to develop decentralized, scalable, efficient and high-impact solutions to the challenges of social innovation (e.g. integrating more democratic and citizen-fair processes). The applications had to address a societal need. This contest was managed by the European Commission's DG Connect[15]. In order to meet the challenge, applicants had to develop software platforms or services, accessible online on the Web or through mobile applications, in the form that best suited the purpose. The rules of this contest stipulated that the solutions presented had to be open source

---

14 More details on the different technology readiness levels: https://www.entreprises.gouv. fr/files/files/directions_services/politique-et-enjeux/innovation/tc2015/technologies-cles-2015-annexes.pdf.

15 DG Connect – Directorate General for Communication Networks, Content and Technology – is the European Commission's department responsible for the European Union's policy on digital, network security, science and digital innovation.

(i.e. available to all, with no intellectual property issues). Five criteria, according to the contest rules (Rules of contest 2018)[16]:

– Social impact: the solution must have a positive social impact. This can be demonstrated and quantified in different ways, depending on the specific topic being addressed: one such measure is the size of the user community actively engaged by the actual implementation.

– Decentralization and governance: the objective here is to contribute to improving transparency and accountability (while respecting privacy and/or anonymity) compared to existing centralized solutions, based on multidisciplinary considerations covering technological (computing, programming, etc.), social (sociology, psychology, art, etc.) and economic (innovation, new business models, etc.) sciences.

– Ease of use and inclusiveness: the proposed solution must be easy to use and affordable and must be able to appeal to the largest number of EU citizens, regardless of their gender, origin, financial capacity or computer skills. Both the user interfaces and the underlying principles will be evaluated.

– Large-scale viability: considered here are cost-effectiveness (including detailed considerations and metrics on energy consumption and environmental impact), solution scalability, security and sustainability models.

– European added value: the added value of the implementation of shown must be clear to European citizens, in terms of novelty, efficiency compared to existing centralized solutions and other societal, economic or environmental aspects.

In 2019, applicants from 43 different countries submitted 178 proposals, including 33 from non-EU countries. Unlike other EC contests, this one allowed non-EU teams to apply. The applicants were mostly small private companies or consortia, as well as individuals and public institutions. Twenty-three proposals were selected by the evaluators to participate in the closing[17] and final jury decision event in February 2020. The evaluators or

---

16 https://ec.europa.eu/research/participants/data/ref/h2020/other/prizes/contest_at/h2020-prizes-rules-bc-social-good_en.pdf.
17 https://www.ngi.eu/event/blockchains-for-social-good/.

members of the jury are experts selected by the organizers of the contest, either from the EC expert base or from their own networks. The projects finally awarded in September 2020[18] provide support in the following areas[19]:

– The quality of content: the Dutch SME WordProof has developed a tool to prove authenticity and make information verifiable.

– Traceability and fair trade: the British social enterprise Project Provenance has developed a tool that allows companies to prove their social impact on supply chains.

– Financial inclusion: GMeRitS, from Finland's Aalto University, is conducting large-scale experiments with alternative economic structures.

– Aid and philanthropy: UnBlocked Cash Project OXBBU by the Irish organization Oxfam and the French start-up Sempo propose a decentralized model for the delivery of international disaster aid.

– The decentralized circular economy: the French cooperative Kleros pro sets up a platform for the resolution of consumer disputes in the field of e-commerce.

– Energy: the Italian company Prosume provides a digital marketplace centralized and autonomous for energy exchanges between peers.

Does this contest meet the expectations of the European Commission towards more openness and inclusiveness and in what way(s)?

The analysis of the contest rules tends to show that the latter presents characteristics of openness and inclusiveness on the following points:

– First, the profile of potential applicants to the competition reflects a broad range. "Individuals, social entrepreneurs, civil society organizations, research centers from technological and social disciplines, creative industries, students, hackers, start-ups and SMEs are invited to apply. Tackling this challenge requires a multidisciplinary expertise" (Rules of Contest 2018)[20]. Multidisciplinarity is thus essential: technological,

---

18 https://www.ngi.eu/news/2020/06/30/blockchains-for-social-good-eic-prize-winners-announced/#winnersselected.

19 https://errin.eu/news/six-winners-named-eic-horizon-prize-blockchains-social-good.

20 https://ec.europa.eu/research/participants/data/ref/h2020/other/prizes/contest_at/h2020-prizes-rules-bc-social-good_en.pdf.

economic, psychological, philosophical, etc., skills can contribute to a solution. Here, the dialogue of disciplines can lead to proposing new solutions and to responding closely to the needs of society.

– Second, to be eligible, applicants must publish their source code via an open source license. Here, the Commission wishes to encourage the opening of solutions and data, for a broader benefit to society. It is important to note that this is the first time that the *open source* criterion has been introduced into the Commission's contest scheme.

– Third, preparatory workshops and the use of community experts were organized before the launch of the contest to specify the needs, the objective, the evaluation criteria. There was an active participation of various stakeholders in the specification of the architecture of the course. The analysis of previous contests tended to show that only the DG members of the Commission concerned defined the properties and characteristics of the contest's operation (Liotard and Revest 2021).

– Fourth, the evaluation process by the jury of experts has also evolved compared to the first European H2020 contests. Indeed, once the competition is over, the experts generally carry out an individual and then a collective evaluation (via a hearing of the selected candidates) and this, according to the evaluation criteria defined beforehand in the rules of the contest. For BCSG, the next step has been added to the process.

In December 2019, the 23 finalists' solutions were published on the BCSG website with the opportunity to comment on each proposal (positive comments, negative comments, pointing out problems that the jury may not have identified):

> So the idea was to present the proposals and get feedback before the final jury. And that's what we did, at the end of December, we published all the finalists' projects […] on the NGI website[21], our website, the website of the project for social good. And there was the possibility of blogging, of putting comments on each proposal, with the aim of helping the jury to evaluate the proposals, taking into account the positive or negative comments made by people, in order to identify

21 DG Connect website: https://www.ngi.eu/.

problems or advantages that the jury had not seen (Interview 1, member of the European Commission).

In February 2020, all applicants presented their applications in poster form not only to the jury members, but also to a large audience (activists, developers, non-governmental organizations). "It was completely open to the public, at one time we had over one hundred and eighty people come to the day" (interview 1). Interactions between the candidates and the public were therefore possible. While the jury members were not able to intervene directly in the discussions, they were able to listen to the presentations and questions in an adjacent room. Afterward, the jury members were able to interview the candidates separately before evaluating them. "And so we kept them in a room right next door with a web stream [...] and each jury member who was involved in a certain area had the opportunity to follow the presentation of these projects, the questions asked by the crowd [...]" (Interview 1, European Commission member).

For the selection of the experts, they were chosen according to the standard Commission process using the DG Connect network and a list of 60,000 potential experts maintained by the European Commission. However, special attention was given to the variety of skills of the experts:

> We already knew who the experts were, or who the people in Europe were rather interested in the societal applications of blockchains, not strictly in the economic applications. So in the experts, there were technological experts, some more oriented towards societal issues, others more interested in economic mechanisms, but always more or less with an in-depth knowledge of at least the possibilities and what had been implemented with blockchain (Interview 1, member of the European Commission).

Thus, the BCSG contest represents a significant advance over previous H2020 contests in that it has contests previously launched within the framework of H2020 insofar as it presents more pronounced properties in terms of openness and inclusiveness. Advances in the constitution of the jury of experts and in the way candidates are selected have been observed.

1.4.2. *Affordable High-Tech for Humanitarian Aid (AHTHA): an attempt to increase cooperation?*

The contest *Affordable High-Tech for Humanitarian Aid* was launched in November 2017 and ended in early 2020. It was jointly piloted by DG *Economic and Social Transitions* and DG *International Cooperation*. The main objective of this competition is to develop low-cost, potentially frugal technological solutions[22], that can be used in humanitarian aid. The targeted technologies are nano-technologies, advanced materials, industrial biotechnology, advanced fabrication in these areas (see contest rules 2017)[23]. The contest is based on potential examples of how these types of technologies can contribute to the needs of people in the Global South, such as: shelters made from advanced materials, portable water filtration and purification using nanotechnology catalysts, off-grid energy supply (organic photovoltaics) or customized humanitarian supplies made in the field using 3D printing technology.

The proposed prize is 5 million euros, which can be divided initially among five winners. The evaluation criteria of the winners are a number of points each, awarded by the jury. The criteria concerned are as follows:

– The new solution must be successfully and safely tested in a real-world environment. Potential for adaptability and scalability in different humanitarian aid contexts must be demonstrated.

– The quality and sustainability properties of the solution based on the frugal application of advanced technologies must be proven.

– The solution must be considered inexpensive and cost-effective (for the beneficiaries and the organizations responding to the crises).

– The winning team must demonstrate engagement with end users, be sensitive to the needs of the most vulnerable (taking into account age, gender, disability and minorities), and have a business case.

---

22 Frugal innovation refers to the search for a low-cost solution, characterized by common sense, and responding to local needs mainly from the South. For further reading: Radjou and Prabhu (2019).

23 https://ec.europa.eu/research/participants/data/ref/h2020/other/prizes/contest_rules/h2020-prizes-eic-rules-high-tech-aid_en.pdf.

The five winners[24] awarded in June 2020 proposed solutions in a variety of areas:

– Shelter and related assistance: the LHP proposal, developed by South African SME Lumkani, is a low-cost solution that alerts the entire community to fires in settlements such as slums or refugee camps.

– Water, sanitation and hygiene: Lorawan, developed by the United Nations High Commissioner for Refugees (UNHCR), provides real-time solutions for remote monitoring of water trucks and tanks to improve the efficiency of water trucking programs worldwide.

– Energy: BRIGHT Move from Norwegian SME Bright Products AS provides refugees with light and energy through an affordable, recyclable and rapidly deployable phone charging device, combined with a solar lantern.

– Health and medical care: TeReFa, developed by the French non-profit organization Handicap International, provides affordable, high-quality prostheses and orthoses produced through 3D scanning and printing technologies.

– Open category: Odyssey2025, developed by the French nonprofit Handicap International, deploys drones to improve the efficiency and safety of land release during demining (enabling land reuse), while reducing costs and ensuring sustainability.

How does this contest respond to the demands of the European Commission towards more openness and cooperation?

The theme and objectives of the contest (to develop frugal technological solutions for humanitarian aid) already have a dimension of inclusiveness: to offer vulnerable populations inexpensive solutions for major needs in terms of health, hygiene, housing, etc. The aim is to include more and more people in accessing these innovations based on frugal technologies (shelter, energy, health, etc.). This integration is also based on new technologies. As Carlos Moedas, Commissioner for Research, Science and Innovation, reminds us: "High technology can have an important inclusive role. Advanced technologies can help more people, especially the most vulnerable, to have

---

24 https://ec.europa.eu/info/news/eic-horizon-prize-affordable-high-tech-humanitarian-aid-commission-awards-five-outstanding-solutions-2020-sep-24_en.

affordable access to sustainable, high-quality products, which will improve their quality of life."[25]

In addition, one of the criteria for evaluating the proposed solutions is based on engagement with end users. Indeed, the rules of the contest specify:

> The solution will be developed through a needs-based approach, defined inclusively with local communities, potential beneficiaries, and organizations responding to crises, and will result as much as possible from cooperation between the private sector, including SMEs, the community of science and research, and humanitarian organizations.

This criterion clearly emphasizes the search for inclusiveness and cooperation.

The cooperation itself takes several forms. First, from the moment the contest is launched, the DG in charge of the contest works with other DGs and humanitarian organizations.

> We had discussions at the time with the management, which was concerned with international cooperation, because for me, in any case, there was clearly an international dimension to frugal innovation. There was a European dimension, of course, but there was clearly a possibility of international cooperation in this sector with this approach, and then we had this idea of humanitarianism. We entered into discussion with DG ECO: it is the DG that deals with humanitarian aid. And so we thought that it could be a good contest because there was a need for innovation. In humanitarian aid in particular, there are increasing needs, increasingly complex situations to manage, more and more people affected, but not necessarily more resources, so this highlights a real need for innovation (Interview 2, European Commission member).

Second, during the reflections on the design and the rules of the contest, two preparatory workshops were organized. Many stakeholders were invited, both internal to the European Commission and external. For the second

---

25 https://ec.europa.eu/echo/node/5178_fr.

workshop, representatives of humanitarian associations, NGOs, Red Cross, UNHCR, Nesta, etc., were invited to refine the rules and criteria for awarding the winners:

> I talked to a lot of people at that time, either about the contests, or about humanitarian aid for the contest, but I think this is very important. I think the part in engagement with stakeholders to define the contest is a crucial part (Interview 2, European Commission member).

In summary, the two European contests tend to show a certain degree of openness and inclusiveness not observed when the first contests were launched in 2015. The openness and inclusiveness are perceived at different levels: at the level of the definition of the subjects and the objectives pursued or at the level of the integration of stakeholders at different stages of the process, during the definition and during the evaluation. More precisely, two forms of inclusiveness can be distinguished. The first concerns the theme of the contest itself and the target audience. A second form refers to the intervention of stakeholders in the process itself. The European contests are a testimony to an inclusiveness of the "first form", and of the beginnings of inclusivity of the second form. These two examples illustrate the desire to reorient, at least in part, the policy of support for European innovation. However, in order to meet the expectations expressed in the 2016 report "Open Innovation, Open Science", it is probably necessary to go further.

1.5. Discussion and conclusion

Reflection on openness must be undertaken to improve the contest process to make it more efficient, to respond to demands for inclusiveness. Even if the two cases presented above tend to show a more voluntary approach towards more cooperation and inclusiveness, efforts are still needed to make the contest process more open. This approach could take two directions. On the one hand, recommendations are to be made to further involve multidisciplinary stakeholders, leading to enriching knowledge. On the other hand, the role of the stakeholders in the construction of the contest, and their continuous and active involvement in the development must also be integrated (Mergel 2020). In the discussion, we want to explore two avenues for improvement: on the one hand, the establishment of co-production mechanisms at all stages of the contest chain, on the other hand, greater use of communities.

1.5.1. *Contests and mechanisms of co-production of knowledge*

Two complementary paths are emerging to address the issue of the implementation of continuous interaction between various stakeholders and the European Commission during the different stages of the contest: the peer production and coproduction processes, on the one hand, and increased attention to the design construction of the contest, on the other hand. Work on OI focusing on the place of peer production and co-production (as concepts included in crowdsourcing) is proving to be extremely stimulating. The notion of commons-based peer production was described by Benkler (2006) and Benker and Nissenbaum (2006). It is not limited to an addition of fragmented and scattered individual knowledge, but refers to a cooperative process of the members of a "crowd" whose actions are oriented towards a specific objective (Mergel 2015). Within public OI systems, the author identifies votes and comments between stakeholders as activities that improve the process. Co-production, on the other hand, focuses on the different forms of collaboration between stakeholders and public actors, the two parties then sharing certain prerogatives with regard to the development of new services, products, programs, etc. Co-production within public OI responds to the following injunction: if innovations are for citizens, they must be developed and implemented in conjunction with them (Bason 2018). Co-creation can even go beyond the framework of improvements and can be mobilized to collectively define the notion of public value (Alves 2013). It can be considered as a guide form that can help structure the involvement of internal and external stakeholders, stimulate the innovation capacities of public actors, and ultimately be the source of change (Bason 2018). Some of the literature on innovation in the public sector has seized on this concept to propose five forms of involvement of stakeholders (including the citizen) in the service production cycle audience (Mergel 2020): co-initiation, co-design, co-implementation, co-delivery and co-evaluation (Surowieki 2004; Lukensmeyer and Torres 2008; Misuraca 2009; Johannessen and Olsen 2010).

While these mechanisms are interesting from a conceptual point of view, putting them into practice can be complex. More specifically, how to initiate peer-production and co-production practices by stakeholders within contests and integrate them effectively in the three stages of the process?

One proposal would be to focus on the design of the contest. Its design is a fundamental step for sponsors, and sponsors should pay special attention to it. Kay (2011, 2012) and Kay et al. (2017) emphasize the following issues when constructing the design: determining the amount and nature of the monetary award, a good knowledge of the participants' motivations, a better evaluation of the results obtained, etc. While Kay is one of the few researchers to insist on the crucial stage of design construction, his analysis and proposals are oriented in a reflection of the criteria that should allow increasing the chances of the contest's success. However, this reflection could be used to support a problematic of inclusiveness: what architecture and what criteria are necessary for a contest to implement peer-production and co-production on an ongoing basis? Contests launched by US federal agencies in the mid-2010s were already showing some signs of openness and inclusiveness (Liotard and Revest 2018)[26].

However, the proposed approach remains marked by a top-down movement: indeed, the collaborative and co-creation initiatives are uniquely initiated by the sponsor of the contest. We propose broadening the reflection to the researching and the setting in motion of more bottom-up processes.

1.5.2. *A reflection on communities of innovation*

Recent research on private OI (West and Sims 2018) identifies three forms of crowdsourcing activities and organizational forms combined: crowds communities, and a third category combining the two (hybrid crowd). If innovation contests are located in the crowd category (a competitive process involving Internet users), the "community" category could help overcome some of the limitations highlighted above, namely the lack of pluridisciplinarity and a single top-down movement initiated and controlled by the sponsor. An innovation community is defined as a network of real interactions between its members, who share a common identity and

26 The Rebuild by Design contest, launched by the US Department of Housing and Urban Development, had as its evaluation criteria the composition of the teams and their ability to collaborate with each other (OST 2011). For the Harvard-NASA Tournament Lab, NASA partnered with the Top Coder platform and Harvard University to access a larger community of developers (Lakhani and Tong 2012).

goals. Communities are characterized by different degrees of openness. Crowds and communities can be regularly or punctually complimentary. Indeed, existing communities may provide a crowd-based mode of problem solving, or crowd participants may develop relationships that lead them to form communities, especially if there are peer-to-peer interactions (Boudreau and Lakhani 2013). According to West and Sims (2018), the coexistence and interweaving over time of communities and crowds can even give rise to a hybrid crowd, a situation that includes both competition elements based on crowd appeal, and community collaboration to help with design or product promotion.

Thus, the crowd/community association would have the following advantages:

– The community created or solicited would thus make it possible to reach a more consequent, more heterogeneous crowd, motivated by the same objectives, but with members having statutes, reputations, expertise and varied knowledge, thus answering the will of more pluridisciplinarity.

– The community could stimulate reflection on many issues: contest topics and rules, evaluation mechanism of the results.

– The community could intervene continuously throughout the process with the capacity, if necessary, to adapt the rules and the temporality of the contest in agreement with the team that would manage the contest.

– Finally, the winners, and especially the losers, could join the community and increase its overall knowledge of the subject concerned. The question of capitalizing on knowledge, especially that produced by the losing teams, was highlighted by Mergel (2015) with regard to contests posted on the Challenge.Gov platform. Identical concerns from our interlocutors appeared for the H2020 innovation contests, with some wondering how to reward also the "good" solutions that were not awarded at the end of the contest.

If the combination of organizational forms, contests and communities seems to us to be a promising path, it is not without obstacles to overcome. The first obstacle is that of adherence to an identity and shared objectives, intrinsic characteristics of the existence of a community. Indeed, the monetary prizes included in the contest mechanisms do not seem sufficient to imply a long-term commitment from the members of the community (Terwiesch and Xu 2008; Boudreau and Lakhani 2009). One avenue is proposed by Langner and Seidel (2015), through two examples involving private companies. The authors highlight practices – such as the realization of joint projects – at the origin of the construction of a dual social identity (between that of the company and that of the community), which allow for a sustainable commitment of members of both organizations. The construction of such an identity could also be imagined at the level of a public organization (such as the EC) and a community. With regard to the innovation contests led by the Commission, we can imagine active bridges with other programs related to innovation and open research.

The second obstacle to overcome in order to achieve an effective association between contest and community would be the mode of governance. Indeed, these two forms of organization are not governed by the same principles. On the one hand, the governance of communities in general is characterized by democratic processes and self-governance (Dahlander et al. 2008). Its goal is most often to encourage individual participation by generating recognition and increased responsibility (O'Mahony and Ferraro 2007; West and O'Mahony 2008). On the other hand, the governance of innovation contest is decided and implemented by the sponsor. Combining the beneficial effects of innovation contests and communities thus requires precise reflection on the appropriate modes of governance. One of the pitfalls mentioned by the interviewees is the conflict of interest for those who would both contribute ideas and also want to participate in the competition. It will then be necessary to think about governance mechanisms that would be adapted to both forms, and flexible enough to take into account the specificity of the themes. An interesting way of thinking about the issue of more malleable modes of governance is proposed by Kuhlmann et al. (2019), through the notion of tentative governance. This form of governance is presented as being limited in time, characterized by trial-and-error processes and learning mechanisms. Thinking of governance as flexible, adaptable and changeable also makes it easier to integrate dimensions such as inclusiveness and reflexivity.

In this chapter, we have shown how a public actor such as the European Commission has taken hold of OI and crowdsourcing issue over the past few years and has reactivated the mechanism of the contest mechanism through its Horizon 2020 program. From DG RTD's digital portal, Europe is following in the footsteps of its American counterpart Challenge.Gov by posting contents including technological as well as societal dimensions. The two case studies highlight the progress of the public sector towards greater openness and inclusiveness of stakeholders. However, there is still a long way to go: as long as the European actor thinks of contests within a pre-established framework, such as the framework programs (Horizon 2020 or Horizon Europe) that define ex ante the future directions of innovation, contests will not be able to claim to take into account the full extent of the criteria of inclusiveness, openness and flexibility that innovation needs. In order to extend the reflection, we propose some lines of research for the future: first, public actors attracted by the "innovation contest" instrument must pay considerable attention to the definition of the architecture of the contest, in order to integrate the dimensions of openness and inclusiveness in a relevant and adequate way. Second, a combination of a contest mechanism and an innovation community (or communities) would increase the share of interdisciplinary knowledge, and ultimately enrich the whole process of creating new ideas, concepts, services or products.

1.6. Acknowledgments

The research leading to these results was supported by the European Union's Horizon 2020 research and innovation program under grant agreement no. 822781 GROWINPRO – Growth Welfare Innovation Productivity.

1.7. References

Adler, J.H. (2011). Eyes on a climate prize: Rewarding energy innovation to achieve climate stabilization. *Harvard Environmental Law Review*, 35(1), 1–45.

Alves, H. (2013). Co-creation and innovation in public services. *The Service Industries Journal*, 33(7–8), 671–682.

Arrona, A. and Zabala-Iturriagagoitia, J.M. (2019). On the study and practice of regional innovation policy: The potential of interpretive policy analysis. *Innovation: The European Journal of Social Science Research*, 32(1), 148–163.

Bason, C. (2018). *Leading Public Sector Innovation 2E: Co–creating for a Better Society*. Policy Press, Bristol.

Bekkers, V. and Meijer, A. (2015). A metatheory of e-government: Creating some order in a fragmented research field. *Government Information Quarterly*, 32(3), 237–245.

Benkler, Y. (2006). *The Wealth of Networks: How Social Production Transforms Markets and Freedom.* Yale University Press, London.

Benkler, Y. and Nissenbaum, H. (2006). Commons-based peer production and virtue. *The Journal of Political Philosophy*, 14(4), 394–419.

Boudreau, K. and Lakhani, K. (2013). Using the crowd as an innovation partner. *Harvard Business Review*, 91(4), 61–69.

Brabham, D.C. (2009). Crowdsourcing the public participation process for planning projects. *Planning Theory*, 8(3), 242–262.

Breul, J.D. (2010). Practitioner's perspective – Improving sourcing decisions. *Public Administration Review*, 70(s1), s193–s200.

Burger-Helmchen, T. and Pénin, J. (2011). Crowdsourcing : définition, enjeux, typologie. *Management Avenir*, 1(41), 254–269.

Chesbrough, H. (2003). The era of open innovation? *MIT Sloan Management Review*, 44(3), 34–42.

Chesbrough, H. (2006). Open innovation: A new paradigm for understanding industrial innovation. In *Open Innovation: Researching a New Paradigm*, Chesbrough, H., Vanhaverbeke, W., West, J. (eds). Oxford University Press, Oxford.

Dahlander, L., Frederiksen, L., Rullani, F. (2008). Online communities and open innovation. *Industry and Innovation*, 15(2), 115–123.

Desouza, K.C. and Mergel, I. (2013). Implementing open innovation in the public sector: The case of Challenge.Gov. *Public Administration Review*, 73(6), 882–890.

Dunleavy, P., Margetts, H., Bastow, S., Tinkler, J. (2006). New public management is dead-long live digital-era governance. *Journal of Public Administration Research and Theory*, 16(3), 467–494.

Eisenhardt, K.M. (1989). Building theories from case study research. *Academy of Management Review*, 14(4), 532–550.

Estellés-Arolas, E. and González-Ladrón-De-Guevara, F. (2012). Towards an integrated crowdsourcing definition. *Journal of Information Science*, 38(2), 189–200.

Etzhowitz, H. (2003). Innovation in innovation: The triple helix of university-industry-government relations. *Social Science Information*, 42(3), 293–337.

Etzkowitz, H. and Leydesdorff, L. (2000). The dynamics of innovation: From national systems and "Mode 2" to a triple helix of university-industry-government relations. *Research Policy*, 29(2), 109–123.

European Commission (2014). Boosting open innovation and knowledge transfer in the European Union [Online]. Available at: https://op.europa.eu/en/publication–detail/–/publication/5af0ec3a–f3fb–4ccb–b7ab–70369d0f4d0c.

European Commission (2016). Open innovation, open science, open to the world. A vision for Europe [Online]. Available at: https://op.europa.eu/fr/publication-detail/-/publication/3213b335-1cbc-11e6-ba9a-01aa75ed71a1.

Fountain, J. (2004). *Building the Virtual State: Information Technology and Institutional Change*. Brookings Institution Press, Washington.

Gassmann, O. and Enkel, E. (2004). Towards a theory of open innovation: Three core process archetypes. *R&D Management Conference*, RADMA, Lisbon.

Gawer, A. (2014). Bridging differing perspectives on technological platforms: Toward an integrative framework. *Research Policy*, 43(7), 1239–1249.

Gonzalez-Fernandez, S., Kubus, R., Pérez–Iñigo, J.M. (2019). Innovation ecosystems in the EU: Policy evolution and horizon Europe proposal case study (the actors' perspective). *Sustainability*, 11(17), 1–25.

Guittard, C. and Schenk, E. (2016). Crowdsourcing et développement d'un écosysteme d'affaires : une étude de cas. *Innovations*, 1(16), 39–54.

Harrison, T.M., Guerrero, S., Burke, G.B., Cook, M., Cresswell, A., Helbig, N., Pardo, T. (2012). Open government and e–government: Democratic challenges from a public value perspective. *Information Policy*, 17(2), 83–97.

Howe, J. (2006). The rise of crowdsourcing. *Wired*, 14.

Huston, L. and Sakkab, N. (2006). Connect and develop: Inside Procter and Gamble's new model for innovation. *Harvard Business Review*, 58–66.

Hutter, K., Hautz, J., Füller, J., Mueller, J., Matzler, K. (2011). Communitition: The tension between competition and collaboration in community-based design contests. *Creativity and Innovation Management*, 20(1), 3–21.

Isckia, T. and Lescop, D. (2011). Une analyse critique des fondements de l'innovation ouverte. *Revue française de gestion*, 210, 87–98.

Janssen, M. and Estevez, E. (2013). Lean government and platform-based governance – Doing more with less. *Government Information Quarterly*, 30, S1–S8.

Johannessen, J.A. and Olsen, B. (2010). The future of value creation and innovations: Aspects of a theory of value creation and innovation in a global knowledge economy. *International Journal of Information Management*, 30(6), 502–511.

Jullien, N. and Pénin, J. (2014). Innovation ouverte : vers la génération 2.0 (Open Innovation: Toward the 2.0 generation). In *Encyclopédie de la Stratégie*, Tannery, F., Denis, J.P., Hafsi, T., Martinet, A.C. (eds). Vuibert, Paris.

Kalil, T. (2006). *Prizes for Technological Innovation*. Brookings Institution, Washington.

Kalil, T. (2012). The grand challenges of the 21st century [Online]. Available at: https://obamawhitehouse.archives.gov/sites/default/files/microsites/ostp/grandch allenges-speech-04122012-rev.pdf.

Kay, L. (2011). Managing innovation prize in government. Report, IBM Center for the Business of Government [Online]. Available at: https://www.businesso fgovernment.org/report/managing-innovation-prizes-government [Accessed 7 February 2022].

Kay, L. (2012). Opportunities and challenges in the use of innovation prizes as a government policy instrument. *Minerva*, 50(2), 191–196.

Kay, L. (2018). The use of innovation prize in government. Science and innovation policy research report [Online]. Available at: https://sih.berkeley.edu/ research–project/the–use–of–innovation–prizes–in–government/.

Kay, L., Conrad, A., Nurayan, T., Geyer, J., Bell, S. (2017). A framework for evaluating innovation challenges. *AgResults* [Online]. Available at: https:// agresults.org/learning/25-a-framework-for-evaluating-innovation-challenges/file.

Kuhlmann, S., Stegmaier, P., Konrad, K. (2019). The tentative governance of emerging science and technology – A conceptual introduction. *Research Policy*, 48(5), 1091–1097.

Lakhani, K.R. and Panetta, J.A. (2007). The principles of distributed innovation. *Innovations: Technology, Governance, Globalization*, 2(3), 97–112.

Lakhani, K. and Tong, R. (2012). Public-private partnerships for organizing and executing prize-based competitions. *Berkman Center Research Publication No. 2012-13* [Online]. Available at: https://papers.ssrn.com/sol3/papers.cfm? abstract_id=2083755 [Accessed 7 February 2022].

Lebraty, J.F. and Lobre-Lebraty, K. (2010). Créer de la valeur par le crowdsourcing : la dyade Innovation – Authenticité. *Systèmes d'information et management*, 15(3), 9–40.

Lebraty, J.F. and Lobre-Lebraty, K. (2013). *Crowdsourcing: One Step Beyond.* ISTE Ltd, London, and John Wiley & Sons, New York.

Liotard, I. and Revest, V. (2018). Contests as innovation policy instruments: Lessons from the US federal agencies' experience. *Technological Forecasting and Social Change*, 127, 57–69.

Liotard, I. and Revest, V. (2021). Open innovation and prizes: Is the European commission really committed? Working document, GROWINPRO working paper, 46/2021.

Lukensmeyer, C.J. and Torres, L.H. (2008). Citizensourcing: Citizen participation in a networked nation. In *Civic Engagement in a Network Society*, Yang, K. and Bergrud, E. (eds). Information Age Publishing, Charlotte.

Lüttgens, D., Pollok, P., Antons, D., Piller, F. (2014). Wisdom of the crowd and capabilities of a few: Internal success factors of crowdsourcing for innovation. *Journal of Business Economics*, 84(3), 339–374.

Makela, A. (2017). Fostering innovation and growth in the digital age: The case for challenge prizes in Europe. Policy brief, College of European [Online]. Available at: http://aei.pitt.edu/93105/.

Masters, A. and Delbecq, B. (2008). Accelerating innovation with prize rewards: History and typology of technology prizes and new contest design for innovation in African agriculture. Working document, International Food Policy Research Institute.

Maurer, S.M. and Scotchmer, S. (2004). *Procuring Knowledge.* Emerald Group Publishing Limited, Bingley.

May, T. (2011). *Social Research: Issues, Methods and Research.* McGraw-Hill, Open University Press, London.

Meijer, A. (2015). E governance innovation: Barriers and strategies. *Government Information Quarterly*, 32(2), 198–206.

Mergel, I. (2015). Opening government: Designing open innovation processes to collaborate with external problem solvers. *Social Science Computer Review*, 33(5), 599–612.

Mergel, I. (2018). Open innovation in the public sector: Drivers and barriers for the adoption of Challenge.Gov. *Public Management Review*, 20(5), 726–745.

Mergel, I. (2020). La co-création de valeur publique par les directions du numérique : une comparaison internationale. *Action publique, recherche et pratique*, 6, 6–16.

Mergel, I., Edelmann, N., Haug, N. (2019). Defining digital transformation: Results from expert interviews. *Government Information Quarterly*, 36(4), 101385.

Misuraca, G.C. (2009). E-Government 2015: Exploring m–government scenarios, between ICT–driven experiments and citizen–centric implications. In *Foresight for Dynamic Organisations in Unstable Environments*, Mendonça, S. and Sapio, B. (eds). Routledge, London.

Murray, F., Stern, S., Campbell, G., MacCormack, A. (2012). Grand innovation prizes: A theoretical, normative and empirical evaluation. *Research Policy*, 41(10), 1779–1792.

Nam, T. (2012). Suggesting frameworks of citizen–sourcing via Government 2.0. *Government Information Quarterly*, 29(1), 12–20.

OECD (2017). Embracing innovation in government global trends [Online]. Available at: https://www.oecd.org/gov/innovative-government/embracing-innovation-in-government.pdf.

Office of Science and Technology (OST) (2011). Implementation of federal prize [Online]. Available at: https://www.challenge.gov/assets/document-library/ FY2011-Implementation-Federal-Prize-Authority-Report.pdf.

O'Mahony, S. and Ferraro, F. (2007). The emergence of governance in an open source community. *Academy of Management Journal*, 50(5), 1079–1106.

Owen, R. and Pansera, M. (2019). Responsible innovation and responsible research and innovation. In *Handbook on Science and Public Policy*, Simon, D., Kuhlmann, S., Stamm, J., Canzler, W. (eds). Edward Elgar Publishing, Cheltenham.

Owen, R., Macnaghten, P., Stilgoe, J. (2012). Responsible research and innovation: From science in society to science for society, with society. *Science and Public Policy*, 39(6), 751–760.

Palacios, M., Martinez-Corral, A., Nisar, A., Grijalvo, M. (2016). Crowdsourcing and organizational forms: Emerging trends and research implications. *Journal of Business Research*, 69(5), 1834–1839.

Penin, J., Burger-Helmchen, T., Guittard, C., Schenk, E., Dintrich, A. (2013). *L'innovation ouverte définition, pratiques et perspectives*. CCI Paris, Paris.

Pisano, G.P. and Verganti, R. (2008). Which kind of collaboration is right for you? *Harvard Business Review*, 86(12), 78–86.

Radjou, R. and Pradhu, J. (2019). *Do Better with Less: Frugal Innovation for Sustainable Growth*. Penguin Random House India Private Limited, New Delhi.

Randhawa, K., Wilden, R., West, J. (2019). Crowdsourcing without profit: The role of the seeker in open social innovation. *R&D Management*, 49(3), 298–317.

Renault, S. (2017). Crowdsourcing : la foule en question(s). *Annales des Mines – Gérer et comprendre*, 3(129), 45–57.

Rochet, J.C. and Tirole, J. (2003). Platform competition in two-sided markets. *Journal of the European Economic Association*, 1(4), 990–1029.

Roson, R. (2005). Two-sided markets: A tentative survey. *Review of Network Economics*, 4(2), 142–160.

Schenk, E. and Guittard, C. (2011). Towards a characterization of crowdsourcing practices. *Journal of Innovation Economics & Management*, 1(7), 93–107.

Scotchmer, S. (2006). *Innovation and Incentives*. MIT Press, Cambridge.

Seidel, V. and Langner, B. (2015). Using an online community for vehicle design: Project variety and motivations to participate. *Industrial and Corporate Change*, 24(3), 635–653.

Sieg, J.H., Wallin, M.W., Von Krogh, G. (2010). Managerial challenges in open innovation: A study of innovation intermediation in the chemical. *R&D Management*, 40(3), 281–291.

Surowiecki, J. (2004). *The Wisdom of Crowds: Why the Many are Smarter than the Few and How Collective Wisdom Shapes Business, Economics, Societies and Nations*. Doubleday, New York.

Tapscott, D. and Williams, A. (2007). *Wikinomics: Wikipédia, Linux, YouTube... Comment l'intelligence collaborative bouleverse l'économie*. Pearson France, Paris.

Terwiesch, C. and Xu, Y. (2008). Innovation contests, open innovation, and multi-agent problem solving. *Management Science, INFORMS*, 54(9), 1529–1543.

Van Eeten, M.J. (2007). Narrative policy analysis. In *Handbook of Public Policy Analysis. Theory, Politics, and Methods*, Fischer, F., Miller, G.J., Sidney, M.S. (eds). CRC/Taylor & Francis, Boca Raton.

Von Hippel, E. (2005). *Democratizing Innovation*. MIT Press, Cambridge.

Weber, M., Lamprecht, K., Biegelbauer, P. (2019). Shaping a new understanding of the impact of Horizon Europe: The roles of the European Commission and Member States. *Fteval Journal for Research and Technology Policy Evaluation*, 47, 146–154.

West, J. and O'Mahony, S. (2008). The role of participation architecture in growing sponsored open source communities. *Industry and Innovation*, 15(2), 145–168.

West, J. and Sims, J. (2018). How firms leverage crowds and communities for open innovation. In *Creating and Capturing Value through Crowdsourcing*, Afuah, A., Tucci, C., Viscusi, G. (eds). Oxford University Press, Oxford.

2

The Regulation of Public Data: The Difficult Case of the Health Sector

If I had to illustrate only one sectoral asset of France in terms of data, and therefore artificial intelligence, it would be the health sector. In the health sector, we know that medical diagnosis, treatment protocols, predictive and preventive medicine are undergoing radical changes. Thanks to artificial intelligence, we are moving towards innovations that will allow us to prevent pathologies, and therefore to drastically reduce the total cost, and to move towards individual medicine, which will also allow us to reduce costs and improve our quality of life and longevity. So, this transformation is absolutely radical and it will affect all sectors of medicine (Translated excerpt from the speech by Emmanuel Macron, President of the Republic, Paris, Collège de France, AI for Humanity, Thursday, March 29, 2018).

Health is thus listed as one of the two priority areas of the French strategic policy on artificial intelligence "AI for humanity" announced in March 2018 following the submission of the report[1] of the parliamentary

Chapter written by Audrey VÉZIAN.

1 Donner un sens à l'intelligence artificielle – Pour une stratégie nationale et européenne. Report, March 2018 [Online]. Available from: https://www.aiforhumanity.fr/pdfs/MissionVillani_Report_ENS-VF.pdf.

mission chaired by Cédric Villani[2]. In the same way as the automotive sector, the other priority area, the health sector is seen as a key area for French economic development. While in the case of the automobile sector, the aim is to "make up for lost time" in "experimentation and development of the autonomous car"[3], in the case of healthcare, the aim is to capitalize on the "massive centralized databases" already created in order to build France's leadership in this field. The forthcoming creation of a national platform for health data (Health Data Hub or HDH), which will centralize access to existing databases and facilitate their use. In addition to the investment of public authorities as high as 1.5 billion over the entire five-year period[4], the establishment of this new organization represents a real break with the policies that have been implemented in this field since the end of the 1990s. While some – notably those belonging to the health industry – see this as a decisive step in the construction of an ecosystem favorable to the economic valorization of health data[5], others (legal researchers, epidemiologists, etc.) are highly critical of the system, which they accuse of not meeting the scientific challenges generated by data sharing (Goldberg and Zins 2021), or they raise numerous questions about the ways in which users of the health system and private and international players will be involved (Bernelin 2019; Bévière-Boyer 2021).

It was in this context, marked by strong divergence around the project, that on January 7, 2022, the French government decided to withdraw the application for operating authorization concerning the HDH from the *Commission nationale informatique et libertés* (CNIL)[6]. This decision, taken following a series of initiatives undertaken over the past 20 years by

---

2 This four-month mission was set up on September 8, 2017 by the Prime Minister, Édouard Philippe, following the #France IA initiative launched under the previous socialist government in March 2017. It was given the task of defining recommendations for the establishment of a national strategy in the field of artificial intelligence.

3 Source: speech by Emmanuel Macron, President of the Republic, Paris, Collège de France, AI for Humanity, Thursday, March 29, 2018.

4 Source: Stratégie nationale de recherche en IA. Press kit, November 28, 2018.

5 Among others, we can cite this recent article published in *Les Echos* entitled "Health data: let's make France a European leader", signed by the French Federation of Health Industries (*Fédération française des industries de santé*), the Alliance for Research and Innovation in the Health Industries (*Alliance pour la recherche et l'innovation des industries de santé*), France Digitale, October 20, 2021.

6 Source: https://www.latribune.fr/technos-medias/informatique/coup-d-arret-pour-le-health-data-hub-la-plateforme-controversee-qui-centralise-les-donnees-de-sante-des-francais-899813.html [Accessed January 7, 2022].

successive governments, demonstrates not only the place occupied by health data on the political agenda but also the importance of this issue for the French government, on the political agenda, but also of its conflictual dimension.

This question about the mode of regulation is all the more acute given that the definition of what is meant by health data is relatively recent (Robin 2021). Indeed, it was not until the law of January 26, 2016 on the modernization of the health system giving rise to the National Health Data System (*Système national des données de santé*, SNDS) for the legislator to explicitly name the different categories of health-related data:

> 1) data from the information systems of public or private health institutions, (2) data from the health insurance national information system, (3) data on causes of death held by local authorities, (4) medico-social data from the departmental houses of disabled people, (5) data on reimbursements by beneficiaries transmitted by complementary health insurance companies (art. L. 1461-1, I CSP) (Robin 2021, p. 34).

This first definition thus refers to data from medico-administrative databases set up for the purpose of managing the healthcare system. Subsequently, the European Regulation on the protection of personal data (GDPR) adopted on April 27, 2016[7] will determine a broad and explicit definition of health data relating to the mental and physical health of an individual, including the provision of healthcare services information about that individual's health. From recital 24 of the regulation, Agnès Robin (2021, p. 35) thus specifies that it is:

> (1) Information about the present or past health 2) information obtained from testing or examination of a body part or bodily substance, including from genetic data and biological examinations; 3) information concerning a disease, disability, risk of disease, medical history, clinical treatment, or physiological or biomedical condition of the individual concerned, regardless of its source.

In fact, the CNIL considers that this includes "certain measurement data from which it is possible to deduce information on the health status of the

---

7 This regulation went into effect on May 25, 2018 in France.

individual"[8]. In other words, in addition to data that "are by their nature related to the state of health of a person (those resulting from the care relationship, for example)", it also concerns "those that would be so, given their destination (such as those resulting from certain connected objects)"[9]. This therefore includes both "classic" medical data and data generated by individuals themselves ("in real life") without any coordination, and collected outside the medical field. This broad conception of health data raises a certain number of questions[10] about the conditions of use (respect for the consent of individuals, etc.) and the methods[11] of making use of this data collected according to various methods and procedures.

This chapter proposes identifying the decisions that give substance to the ambitions of a public policy on data in the health sector and the objectives that accompany them. Such an approach, focused on the forms of regulation of health data, will lead to highlighting the tensions that run through the public sphere and how they influence the choice of public action mechanisms. More generally, it is a question of feeding the reflection on the change of governmental regime introduced by the support given to the structuring, circulation and exploitation of data in the health field: how can the accumulation of data and the increased interconnection of databases contribute to a transformation of the modes of participation of the various stakeholders (citizens, health professionals, public authorities, private actors, etc.)? In order to identify the regulation of health data in France, we have carried out a survey of public decisions on this subject by consulting the websites of the French government and the presidency of the Republic (Ministry of Health, Ministry of Economy, etc.) and those of the institutions and administrations concerned with digital health policy (*Direction de la recherche, des études, de l'évaluation et des statistiques,* Directorate of Research, Studies, Evaluation and Statistics – DREES, *Direction générale des entreprises* (Directorate General of Enterprises) – DGE) as well as a review of the various public and private reports produced in support of these interventions. We also

---

8 Source: CNIL website accessed on November 24, 2021 [Online]. Available at: https://www. cnil.fr/fr/quest-ce-ce-quune-donnee-de-sante.

9 Source: Opinion of the CNIL, following a referral from the Minister of Social Affairs and Health quoted in *Colloque Big Data en santé – Quels usages? Quelles solutions?*, ministère des Affaires sociales et de la Santé, Paris, July 4, 2016, 6.

10 For further development, we refer the reader to Bernelin (2019).

11 They require diverse and varied skills from heterogeneous disciplinary fields: medical, computer, mathematical and statistical (Goldberg and Zins 2021).

systematically explored newspaper archives (*Le Monde, Les Echos*) and the specialized press (TicSanté, TicPharma, APMNews). This approach made it possible to identify the main actions undertaken around health data. In order to clarify the main points of view of the various stakeholders initiatives taken by the public authorities, this survey was also based on semi-structured interviews with representatives of the health administration and organizations in charge of data regulation and participation in seminars with representatives of the HDH, the *Délégation ministérielle du numérique en santé,* the Ministerial delegation of digital health (DNS).

2.1. Tenfold attraction for health data, new digitized tools: towards truly innovative practices?

While the appeal of health data is inherent to medical practice (see section 2.1.1), it has been reinforced by the effect of new technologies which have consequently broadened their parameter and likewise their use (see section 2.1.2). However, paradoxically, it is more a question of dressing up old reformist actions in innovative clothes (see section 2.1.3).

2.1.1. *A constant quest for data*

Health data have always been a challenge for the health sector. The history of medicine was characterized very early on by a desire to bring together different categories of information (lifestyle, environment, clinical signs, family history, etc.) with the aim of better understanding the appearance and disease progression. The search for a combination of various factors has been accompanied concomitantly by the development of new approaches to categorization, storage and visualization of the collected elements. Among others, we can mention the medical nomenclatures framing the anatomical observations, or the epidemiological registers gathering in a continuous and exhaustive way nominative data of one or more health events within a geographically defined population[12]. Thus, many clinical and epidemiological research projects have been a considerable source of data production (Zins et al. 2021).

More broadly, the creation of databases is a classic approach in research on the living (Leonelli 2014). Throughout the 20th century, the production

---

12 Source: Comité d'évaluation des registres.

and integration of data of a varied nature (molecular data of all kinds, clinical picture, etc.) and on a large scale in databases constituted the source of new decisive biological knowledge in the development of clinical techniques and practices to preserve and restore human health. This may be data collected via various media (among others, the patient's medical file within the healthcare establishment, medical examinations carried out by healthcare professionals registered in laboratory management systems, etc.). In addition, if databases are essential for observing, evaluating and improving the health of individuals, it should also be emphasized that they are essential as tools making it possible to shape the dynamics of collaboration and cooperation between different categories of actors (Dagiral and Peerbaye 2013).

2.1.2. Health data with an increasingly broad scope

A multiplication of these databases will take place under the effect of the progress made in molecular biology and the development of new technological tools. The latter – increasingly rapid and less costly – have contributed to the explosion of new data (known as omics) relating to the genetic information of individuals, opening the way to what is known as personalized (or precision) medicine. In addition to the production of new biological data, there are also new sources of data generated by mobile health applications, connected objects or even traces left on the Internet via search engines or social networks, all of which are health indicators captured from the real life of individuals.

Beyond the biomedical sector in the strict sense of the term, many public health data are generated by the State to facilitate the conduct of public action (Chevallier and Cluzel-Métayer 2018). The monitoring of the health of populations has long been at the heart of the preoccupations and political strategies of States, and is a powerful lever for rationalizing the processes of collecting and analyzing health-related data. The construction of the welfare state has made a decisive contribution to accelerating and intensively increasing the production of data in order to provide a precise and systematized account of all traces of use of the healthcare system.

In France, this approach resulted in the creation in 1998 of the *Système national d'information interrégime de l'Assurance maladie* (Sniiram). This first data repository systematically collects information from the reimbursements made by all the health insurance schemes for care in the private sector. This tool therefore brings together individual data concerning both the care recipient and their prescribing doctor(s), as well as information relating to the consumption of care (date of care, coding of examinations carried out, etc.)[13].

Subsequently, the digitalization of information systems in public and private hospital establishments[14], and more broadly, in healthcare organizations (town practices, radiology centers, etc.) and patient records are contributing to an unprecedented massification of health data production within the healthcare system.

2.1.3. Health data used to serve a reform rhetoric that is not very innovative

The development of new analytical treatments (data mining[15], etc.) will contribute to the increased attractiveness of this health data. Indeed, the production of large volumes of constantly updated data is perceived as a way to generate new information on health (among others, Polton 2018; Zins et al. 2021), notably by combining databases from various sources and collected for specific purposes. Digital data will therefore be considered, well beyond the health domain alone (Chevallier and Cluzel-Métayer 2018), as "one of the key factors in the economic and social development" of States. The result is support for actions to structure and homogenize data and their transmission methods, and more broadly for the digitalization of medical activity.

In this context, the reforms of the French healthcare system, and in particular those concerning the hospital sector, are thus ineluctably reflected in the central place given to digital tools, regardless of the partisan

---

13 For more details, we refer the reader to the Health Insurance website: https://assurance-maladie.ameli.fr/etudes-et-donnees/presentation-snds/presentation-systeme-national-donnees-sante-snds.

14 These include the launch in 2011 of the 2012–2016 Digital Hospital (*Hôpital numérique*) program aimed at modernizing and structuring hospital information systems, which was followed by the HOP'EN 2019–2022 program (*Hôpital numérique ouvert sur son environnement*) and then the SUN-ES program (*Ségur usage numérique en établissements de santé*) launched following the Segur health program in 2021.

15 A method of data exploration that allows the analysis of large volumes of data in order to deduce relationships and links between them. The objective is to transform this data into understandable and exploitable information.

orientation of the government. For example, the *e-santé 2020* (e-health 2020) plan launched in July 2016 by the Minister of Health, Marisol Touraine, who mentions in her presentation speech that she wants to "[...] seize all the opportunities of digital technology to make our [health] system more flexible and efficient". Or the provisions made under Workstream 3 "Accelerating the digital shift" of the *Ma santé 2022* (My health 2022) plan launched by the government of Édouard Philippe in September 2018, for which the Minister of Health, Agnès Buzyn, states:

> Digital technologies are bringing about major changes in the organization and functioning of the health system. They should make it possible not only to modernize the current organizations by improving the daily lives of professionals, but also to promote innovative care by strengthening the quality of care for the patient[16].

Until the end of the 2010s, the expected benefits remained confined to the health field and displayed the ambition to "strengthen the efficiency of public policies and health democracy and to bring together the promotion of health, care prevention and the national and regional levels" (Devillier 2017). A careful analysis of the arguments supporting its deployment shows that they are in line with those mobilized during previous health system reforms. Indeed, we note that the injunction to redesign the existing framework in order to integrate the expected/hoped-for/desired contributions of digital technology is based on a number of observations (aging population, increase in chronic diseases, need for a controlled budgetary policy, fight against health inequalities, etc.) identified during previous attempts to reform the health system which have taken place since the 1970s:

> The national health strategy (*La stratégie nationale de santé*, SNS) aims to re-found the health care system by adapting it to the challenges of tomorrow: growing social inequalities in health, adequately coordinated care paths in a system structured more for acute problems than for chronic situations, and finally, solidarity-based financing that must be preserved[17].

16 Source: mission letter from the Minister of Health, project 3 "*Accélérer le virage numérique*" (Accelerating the digital shift) addressed to Dominique Pon and Annelore Coury, March 9, 2018.
17 Letter of referral to the CNNum from Marisol Touraine, Minister of Health dated February 26, 2014.

The ambition of this strategy to transform our health system is precisely to combine our insurance tradition: with the new health needs of our fellow citizens, with new opportunities – I am thinking of technological innovation, scientific, or organizational; as to new constraints – whether budgetary or demographic [...] Built at a time when the priority objective was to respond to acute pathologies for French people who were dying young or were victims of trauma, the French health system must now cope with the aging of the population and the explosion of chronic diseases[18].

Moreover, the levers of action that would result from the exploitation of digital technologies seem, in the end, less original than they appear. In fact, they are very much in line with the steps of a rationalizing enterprise aimed at health professionals. This policy consists of playing on the division of labor and on the modes of cooperation between health professionals in the name of taking better account of patients' needs (Castel and Vézian 2018):

The transformation of our health system cannot take place without a massive and coherent development of digital health in France. Digital is not an end in itself. It is a way to better coordinate health professionals, to develop therapeutic and organizational innovations, to fight against the health divide, to reposition the citizen at the heart of the health system, in short to provide better care[19].

By remedying what is considered to be insufficient integration of their practices (which would be both a source of wasted public funds and a loss of chance of recovery for the patient), digital technologies, understood in the broadest sense (telemedicine platforms, shared medical records, etc.), are seen as a means of increasing skills, facilitating the dissemination of good practices and directing patients to teams with expertise in a specific field. In short, they are being used as one of several instruments to respond to a recurring injunction for professionals to coordinate more and strengthen their collaborative practice in order to improve the quality of the service provided

18 Speech to launch the "Stratégie de transformation du système de santé" (Strategy for Transforming the Healthcare System) by Agnès Buzyn, Minister of Health, March 9, 2018.
19 Roadmap "Accélérer le virage numérique". Information file Ministerial Conference, Paris, April 25, 2019, p. 4.

to the patient (Robelet 2001). Similarly, the use of digital tools as a factor of empowerment for citizen-patients is in line with the actions undertaken to implement health democracy since the beginning of the 2000s. While it is clear that access, collection and sharing of health data are now more facilitated, the examples put forward by its promoters (among others; Polton 2018) say – as in the past – little about the mechanisms by which the information collected would be likely to strengthen the participation of the patient-citizen in health decisions, and more broadly to influence the healthcare system[20]. However, previous work on the concept of the lay expert (Dalgalarrondo 2004) has shown the variability of patients' expertise according to the social configuration in which it is deployed, and the weight of the environment in understanding the real forms of health democracy. In other words, we need to pay closer attention to the extent of the movement to transform public action, which would enable patients and users to play a more active role, and more generally to the concrete effects of digital technologies on the quality and continuity of care.

If this abundance of health data in France (Zins et al. 2021), fueled by a sustained digital policy, potentially opens the way to a transformation of the healthcare system, on the other hand, the emergence of considerable economic stakes attached to the production and use of health data appears to be indisputable.

2.2. Towards an economic valuation of health data in the name of a sovereignty imperative

The impact of the technological boom is not limited to issues related to the transformation of the healthcare system. It was very early on – and perhaps more so – perceived as a determining lever of a "digital health" (or digital) sector presented as an essential element of growth (see section 2.2.1). The significance of this economic issue leads to the establishment of a close public–private consultation around the forms of regulation of health data (see section 2.2.2).

---

20 In particular, little is known about the actual conditions that would lead to a reduction in informational asymmetry in the care relationship between patients and health professionals.

2.2.1. *Public action and data representation as an economic issue*

In the early 2010s, access to health data remained an issue that was primarily the prerogative of the Ministry of Health (the Ministry set up an Open Data Commission for Health in November 2013). While economic perspectives are present in the initiatives undertaken[21], the main focus is on an Open Data policy aimed at modernizing public action[22]. At the same time, we note nevertheless that the issue of economic development around health, and its declination in the digital sector, is increasingly becoming a reason legitimizing public action. We can cite in particular the three "health" plans of France's reindustrialization program ("digital health", "medical devices and new health equipment" and "medical biotechnology") set up in September 2013 by the President of the French Republic, François Hollande, and Arnaud Montebourg, Minister for Productive Restructuring. These three initiatives aim to support industrial projects in personalized medicine, as well as connected medical devices, in order to gain market share internationally in these areas deemed to be promising[23]. While digitalized tools are one of the main drivers of this proactive policy, the prospect of economic development that would result from the exploitation of data is absent. However, since that time, a certain number of reports commissioned by the public authorities[24] mention:

---

21 Source: Mission letter addressed to F. Von Lennep and P. Burnel for the *Commission Open Data en santé*, October 17, 2013.

22 This policy of transformation and modernization of the State has led public authorities to implement a proactive policy of opening up all its public data in order to make them accessible, to promote their circulation and their reuse (Chevallier 2018). Through increasing the openness of medico-administrative data, the aim is to encourage their use either by pooling them or by linking them with other thematic databases outside health in order to facilitate the development of Big Data processing (ministère des Affaires sociales et de la Santé, 2016, p. 2).

23 Source: https://www.economie.gouv.fr/presentation-nouvelle-france-industrielle [Accessed November 15, 2021].

24 Among others, we can cite the report of the mission chaired by Philippe Lemoine, president of the Forum d'action modernités and president of the *Fondation internet nouvelle génération*, entitled "*Transformation numérique de l'économie*" published in November 2014. This mission was jointly requested in January 2014 by the Ministry of Economy and Finance (Pierre Moscovici), the Ministry of Productive Recovery (Arnaud Montebourg) and the Ministry in charge of small- and medium-sized enterprises, innovation and the digital economy (Fleur Pellerin). The report was submitted to Emmanuel Macron, then Minister of the Economy, Industry and Marylise Lebranchu, Minister of Decentralization, Civil Service and State Reform.

– the strategic challenge of "opening up public and corporate data (Open Data) as well as mass processing analytical systems" to support innovation[25];

– or the potential benefits likely to be derived from health data, and in particular from existing medico-administrative databases such as that of Sniiram. It is mentioned in particular that greater accessibility to health data would have direct consequences in terms of innovation (crowdsourcing), by promoting the appearance of new services and products from private players. The economic benefits identified remain, however, confined to the academic sphere (in terms of improving the competitiveness of research), to that of public health (in terms of the organization of the supply of care), or even in terms of controlling the budgetary costs associated with the health policy.

In other words, the question of the uses and exploitation of data remains circumscribed to the biomedical field, and as such, is under the control of the Ministry of Health, and to a lesser extent of the Secretary of State for the research.

Over the years, the representation of health data as an economic issue in its own right will gradually emerge, thanks to the political agenda of artificial intelligence (AI), in a context where the positioning of health as an industrial issue will consolidate[26]. The development and/or improvement of existing artificial intelligence techniques (e.g. the deep neural network) are key elements in the transformation of the use of databases in the French healthcare system. This new attraction to artificial intelligence tools, based on the improvement in computing speed and the increase in available memory, coupled with a profusion of data, will lead to a political reappropriation of the issue surrounding health data and to an evolution in the organization of access to it. Beyond the proper dynamics to research in

---

25 Source: Délégation ministérielle à l'intelligence économique du Premier ministre. Intelligence économique. Report, June 2015, p. 14.

26 We are referring here to the "*Médecine du futur*" (Medicine of the Future) plan, which resulted from the merger in May 2015 of the three former health plans of France's reindustrialization program: *Nouvelle France industrielle* (New Industrial France), mentioned above, under the joint responsibility of Emmanuel Macron, Minister of the Economy, Industry and Digital, the Minister of Social Affairs, Health and Women's and Women's Rights, Marisol Touraine, and the Secretary of State for Higher Teaching and Research, Thierry Mandon.

the field of artificial intelligence invoking the need to make access to health data more flexible[27], this reappropriation is the result of a multiform dynamic. First of all, we see the formalization of a community of private interests centered on the contribution of Big Data to health. Alongside France Biotech, a professional association bringing together representatives of start-ups specializing in health innovation created in 1997 to relay the potential in terms of economic growth of the e-health sector, other organizations have emerged over the 2010s under the impetus of major industrial groups operating in various fields of activity: for example, the Healthcare Data Institute, an association founded in 2014 – among others – by a subsidiary of a telecoms group (Orange Healthcare) and the pharmaceutical group Sanofi, has set itself the mission "to exchange and work on the value of data, their uses and exchanges, digital products and services related to health, Big Data technologies, the transformation of organizations and human resources"[28]. Or the action led by representatives of the insurance sector who interacted during the 2010s to change the representation of the Big Data issue in the insurance sector (Aubry 2017). Through their actions, these different organizations will contribute to positioning health data as an unavoidable issue in the public arena (questioning public authorities by producing memos[29], etc.).

From this perspective, we note the significant activity of consulting firms (among others, Roland Berger, McKinsey & Company, Boston Consulting Group-BCG), which, on the one hand, have developed a whole rhetoric around the economic potential of the digital health market, which has been taken up in studies commissioned by the public authorities or written in

---

27 The promoters of artificial intelligence research point out the obstacles to the development of artificial intelligence tools in health linked to the obligation of non-identification of the patient, which limits the cross-checking of information throughout the patient's care, and the difficulty of justifying the public interest in exploiting data upstream of the exploration and experimentation of said data. Source: https://www.aiforhumanity. fr/pdfs/MissionVillani_Report_ENS-VF.pdf.

28 Source: association statutes: https://healthcaredatainstitute.com/wp-content/uploads/2016/05/statutes_healthcare-data-institute_vdef-14-04-2016.pdf [Accessed February 27, 2022].

29 Among the latest actions are the Health Data Care Institute's proposals to the 2022 presidential candidates. https://healthcaredata institute. com/wp-content/uploads/2021/11/position-paper-hdi-day-2021-citizens-and-health-data-1.pdf.

collaboration with public bodies, and, on the other hand, they have enlisted the services of former political leaders on the subject[30].

The analysis notes produced by consulting firms play an important role in formulating the issues and quantifying the economic prospects attached to the development of digital health and the use of health data.

The involvement of consulting firms can also be more direct, by participating in the drafting of content for public authorities. This is notably the case for Roland Berger, which worked with a group of public and private experts. Its work consisted of identifying "markets of the future" and characterizing these markets and France's competitive advantages in detail. It is thus specified that "the acceleration strategy (in digital health) focuses on the following objectives: 30% of the European market by 2025 (i.e., approximately €30 billion in revenues according to the Roland Berger study); a minimum threefold increase in the number of jobs by 2025 (i.e., approximately 13,000 additional jobs); and the contribution in a measurable way to the shift to ambulatory care and to the efficiency of healthcare spending (e.g., containing the growth of medical transportation to 2%/year)"[31]. In addition to the purely economic aspects, they are also involved in developing and/or relaying political arguments. We think in particular of the stakes in terms of sovereignty In addition to this economic potential, Health Tech companies have a role to play in the reindustrialization and sovereignty policy of Europe[32]. This issue is conditioned in particular by access to data: "To support this development, access to health data is essential and enables the exploitation of the potential of artificial intelligence, and Europe has the opportunity to invent a digital health model that is compatible with its personal data requirements."[33]

Box 2.1. *Influence of consulting firms*

The work done by McKinsey & Company for the *Institut Montaigne* report published in June 2020 is a first example. The arguments, figures and

---

30 This refers to the recruitment of Axelle Lemaire, former Secretary of State for Digital Technology and Innovation from April 2014 to February 2017, to the Roland Berger firm between February 2018 and January 2022.

31 Source: Collège d'experts, 2020, p. 37.

32 Source: BCG, BPIFrance, BioUp, Francebiotech. Plan Healthtech. Du vivier aux grandes réussites, April 13, 2021, p. 13.

33 Source: BCG et al. 2021, p. 18.

diagrams supporting this work are repeated as they were in the Picard report produced by the *Conseil général de l'économie* in April 2021 for the Minister of Industry, in order to inform the e-health access strategy:

> The development potential of the [digital health] sector is deemed 'high'. The development of e-health is likely to bring at least 16 to 22 billion euros in performance gains to the financing of the healthcare system in France, on an annual basis. These gains can be realized in five areas [patient empowerment, data dematerialization and exchange, telemedicine, automation, transparency and decision support] that will create the system of the future[34].

This is how health data will progressively not only become a real issue of economic and industrial sovereignty for public authorities, but will also be the subject of an increasingly close partnership between public and private institutions via the establishment of hybrid working groups around structuring projects[35], and the contractualization of reciprocal commitments on the subject.

2.2.2. Towards public–private co-regulation of health data

To illustrate this evolving issue around health data exploitation, a quick analysis of the actions undertaken by the two main consultative bodies bringing together government and industry representatives, notably the *Conseil stratégique des industries de santé* (CSIS)[36] and the *Comité*

---

34 Source: Picard, 2021, p. 17.

35 We are thinking here of the various working groups ("Valorization of shared data and economic model of the Health Data Hub etc.) set up within the *Alliance pour la recherche et l'innovation des industries de santé* (ARIIS), which brings together representatives of the State (DREES, DGE, DGRI) and industry representatives around the Artificial Intelligence and Health program, which is part of the strategic contract for the healthcare industry and technology sector.

36 Initially set up in 2004 under the auspices of the Prime Minister, the CSIS brings together the ministers responsible for industry research and health and six heads of pharmaceutical and biotechnology companies. Its composition varies over time and according to a random frequency (nine editions have been held since 2004). It is responsible for identifying priority themes and defining the means to be implemented to maintain and strengthen France's attractiveness in the health sector.

stratégique de la filière des industries et des technologies de santé[37] (CSF), presented as complementary[38], is particularly revealing.

Absent from the major actions undertaken in the first three editions held between 2004 and 2012, health data will not only be the subject of increasing interest from these boards, but there is also a widening scope of interest around health data. During the 4th and 5th editions, the health data produced in the medico-administrative and clinical framework are targeted. The issue of their accessibility is clearly limited to the field of pharmaco-epidemiology research.

Starting with the 6th edition, health data becomes an interdisciplinary issue for the healthcare industry. In addition to the field of pharmaco-epidemiology research, they are presented as a major source of therapeutic innovation, and as a decisive element in industrial development and in monitoring the efficiency of health policies.

In this context, the measures will be much more specific and will cover a wide range of issues: increasing the production of health data in relation to clinical activity and their interoperability; structuring and organizing health data and clarification of access to it; legal issues in the context of international competition.

Nevertheless, while the expected benefits in terms of innovation and health policies are positive, there is clear mention of the risks involved in using indirectly identifiable data.

---

37 Created in March 2013, it brings together companies in the human and veterinary medicine, medical device, medical diagnostics, biotechnology and e-health sectors, as well as employee unions and the professional bodies concerned. This committee is the place within which a sector contract is drawn up identifying the key challenges of the sector and the reciprocal commitments of the State and the industrialists, to issue proposals for concrete actions and monitor their implementation. Source: https://www.economie.gouv.fr/signature-contrat-strategique-filiere-industries-et-technologies-sante [consulted on February 23, 2022].

38 Some reports from the CSIS – like the 6th edition – can thus be produced in consultation.

Key themes	Targeted measures
1) Investment fund in the field of health biotechnologies. 2) Employment and training policy. 3) Boosting intelligence gathering and intelligence and repression of trafficking in of counterfeit medicines. 4) Increased partnership research in the biomedical field. 5) The National Alliance for life sciences and health interlocutor of industrialists. 6) Development of bioproduction. 7) Opening up the capital of the biotechnology subsidiary of the *Laboratoire français du fractionnement et des biotechnologies*. 8) Incentive mechanism for the activity manufacturing of pharmaceutical specialties. 9) Reporting of export sales and territoriality of domestic prices. 10) Developing epidemiology in France. 11) Improving access to therapies.	Measures taken within the framework of topic 10: create a portal describing the content of existing private and public health databases and cohorts (nature of the data, contact details of the holders, conditions of access) in compliance with the legislative and regulatory provisions in force, particularly with regard to intellectual property and data protection. Access to these databases will make it possible to carry out specific analyses to better define the target populations for drugs, as well as the risks associated with their use (the analysis of a specific cohort has thus made it possible to define the women most likely to benefit from anti-osteoporosis treatment; a cohort of very premature babies has made it possible to study the long-term consequences of the use of analgesics, etc.); to define management methods, to identify the risks associated with the use of drugs; define management methods, a financing method and harmonized rules for access to the various health databases. Of particular interest is the database of socially insured persons, which includes information on consumers of care and medicines as well as data on pathologies through hospitalizations and long-term illnesses. It is a unique database in Europe to carry out pharmaco-epidemiological studies. The framework for access to this database for epidemiological purposes must be defined.

Table 2.1. *Measurements during the 4th edition – October 2009*

Subsequently, in the 7th edition, this distinction between anonymous and re-identifiable data is no longer mentioned, and it is the request for an opening to all the data that is claimed. Indeed, the accessibility of data is pointed out as a persistent difficulty that needs to be remedied[39].

---

39 Source: it should be noted that these criticisms are recurrent and come from actors not directly concerned by the policy implemented in the pharmaceutical industry. In this perspective, we can cite in particular the tribune published in *Le Monde* on September 27, 2016 signed by Didier Sicard, professor of medicine, honorary president of the *Comité consultatif national d'éthique* and Jean-Marie Spaeth, honorary president of the Caisse *nationale d'Assurance maladie des travailleurs salariés* and honorary president of the *École nationale supérieure de Sécurité sociale*.

Key themes	Targeted measures
1) Strengthening research partnerships. 2) Structuring the health industry sector. 3) Valuing our assets in the globalization process. 4) Anticipating changes in care procedures.	Measure 2 "Strengthen translational and clinical research" taken within the framework of theme 1: work on the publication of a good practice guide for public–private research collaborations including the modalities of access to clinical data and/or biological resources. Measure 3 "Strengthen France's commitment to excellence in pharmaco-epidemiology" taken within the framework of theme 1: facilitate the implementation of studies using data from the Sniiram database and the PMSI.

Table 2.2. *Measurements during the 5th edition – January 2012*

This observation appears paradoxical[40], if we look at the various measures taken by the Ministry of Health under Marisol Touraine's term of office since 2013: establishment of a health data administrator[41] to coordinate the actions of its administrations in relation to administrations in line with the Open Data policy promoted by the General Data Administrator "in terms of inventory, governance, production, circulation and exploitation of data"[42], creation of the National Health Data System (*Système national des données de santé*, SNDS) presented by the French government as a relaxation of access to anonymous and nominative (or indirectly nominative) databases, for all actors, including representatives of private for-profit organizations.

Through this increased openness of medico-administrative data, the aim was to encourage their exploitation either by pooling them or by linking them with other non-health databases in order to facilitate the development of "Big Data" processing[43].

---

40 We will return to the reasons for this paradoxical finding in the third part of this contribution.

41 Source: speech by Marisol Touraine, Minister of Social Affairs and Health. Présentation de la stratégie e-santé. July 4, 2016.

42 Source: art. 2 of Decree No. 2014-1050 of September 16, 2014, establishing a general data administrator.

43 Source: ministère des Affaires sociales et de la Santé, Stratégie nationale e-santé 2020. Le numérique au service de la modernisation et de l'efficience du système de santé. July 4, 2016, p. 17.

Key themes	Targeted measures
1) Research, innovation and training. 2) Health, health efficiency and therapeutic progress. 3) Employment, competitiveness, production. 4) Exportation.	Measure 6 "Structuring and professionalization of clinical research" taken within the framework of theme 1: continue and amplify the structuring of national investigation networks (as far as possible themselves components of pan-European networks), in order to ensure, among other things, the quality of data, patient care and a single entry portal. Measure 9 "Intellectual property: strengthening France's role internationally" taken within the framework of theme 1: coordinating the position of industry and the State on the importance of protecting intellectual property rights in the health sector (trademarks, patents and regulatory data protection) in order to prevent the deterioration of their protection in certain foreign countries (Argentina, India, China, Vietnam, etc.). Measure 10 "Intellectual property: harmonization and simplification of procedures" taken within the framework of theme 1. Measure no. 21 "Administrative simplification: a single regulatory register for medicinal products and a single regulatory register for medical devices at the European level" taken within the framework of theme 2: for medical devices, support Article 53 of the proposal for a European regulation and of the Council on medical devices published on September 26, 2012, which proposes the establishment, in collaboration with the Member States and the European Commission, of a European database that is interoperable with the database on clinical trials of medicinal products for human use for clinical investigations carried out on medical devices. Measure #28 "Promote an active approach to facilitate access to health data for public health, research and research and industrial development" taken within the framework of theme 2.

Table 2.3. *Measurements of the 6th edition*

At the same time, the economic development challenge associated with health data is growing. Not only is the production and use of health data presented as information elements that can increase the quality and performance of the pharmaceutical industry, but health data is now positioned as an economic sector in their own right ("creating a health data economy, a growth factor for all the players involved"). This is reflected in the fact that, for the first time, this subject is being singled out as a major theme or orientation of the CSIS.

Created by the law of modernization of the health system of January 26, 2016, this system brings together the main existing public health databases[44]. It thus assembles "in a single database the health-related information of 66 million French people" (Devillier 2017, p. 58). Access to it is authorized, on a permanent basis, for State services, public establishments and organizations responsible for a public service mission appearing on a list established by decree in the Council of State, and, after authorization issued by the CNIL, for processing implemented by other public or private actors, pursuing research, study or evaluation purposes of public interest[45]. The assessment of public interest is carried out via a "one-stop shop", the *Institut national des données de santé* (INDS), bringing together representatives of the State, obligatory insurers, supplementary insurers, users of the health system, healthcare professionals and structures, representatives of research and teaching, agencies involved in regulation and public health, industries and health product companies as well as research consultancies and service companies[46]. Access to the SNDS is thus conditional on the purpose of the exploitation, and no longer on the legal status of the applicant[47] (Aubry 2017).

Box 2.2. *The National Health Data System*
(Système national des données de santé)

The actions of the last two CSISs have focused on training needs related to the digitization of data, on continuing to structure the accessibility of health data (enrichment, processing and creation of a dedicated infrastructure, the HDH) and their development. The last CSIS consecrated digital health as one of the priority areas of action with dedicated funding,

---

44 As a reminder, these are data from the Sniiram, the PMSI, the *Centre d'épidémiologie sur les causes médicales de décès de l'institut national de santé et de la recherche médicale* (CépiDC), medico-social data from the information system of the *maisons départementales des personnes handicapées* and the *Caisse nationale de solidarité pour l'autonomie*, as well as a "representative sample of reimbursement data per beneficiary transmitted by complementary health insurance organizations and defined in consultation with their representatives". Source: Étude d'impact du projet de loi relatif à l'organisation et à la transformation du système de santé, February 13, 2019.

45 Source: Article L. 1461-1 and L. 1461-3-I, Public Health Code.

46 Source: Article L. 1462-1, Public Health Code.

47 However, the law prohibits the use of the data contained in this file for the promotion of health products and for the purpose of excluding coverage from insurance contracts or modifying insurance contributions and premiums. Source: CNIL: https://www.cnil.fr/snds-systeme-national-des-donnees-de-sante [Accessed on May 11, 2021].

and the signature of a sector contract in December 2020 (supplemented by an amendment in June 2021 following the 9th CSIS), in which artificial intelligence in health is one of the priority themes in connection with the implementation of the HDH.

Key themes	Targeted measures
1) Facilitating patient access to innovations. 2) Valorizing the production. 3) Developing clinical research and open access to health data. Creating the right conditions for the development of data-driven health research as a factor of attractiveness for France. Access to health data is a key strategic issue for research in France (international attractiveness), for health professionals (monitoring of public health indicators), for industry (responding to requests from health authorities, research and innovation), for all actors operating in the health field and for patients and citizens (development of new services) [...]. Ultimately, these advances will create a health data economy which will be a growth factor for all the players involved. 4) Strengthening the State–industry dialogue.	Measure no. 12 taken within the framework of theme 3: an interface between the national platform and the health industry will be set up to define the practical and legal aspects of access to databases.

Table 2.4. *Measures in the 7th edition – April 2016 (Mr. Valls' government)*

In the context of a globalized economy, the issue of health data – and, more broadly, the data policy[48] – is thus evoked as an issue of national and even European sovereignty by all the stakeholders[49]. The Covid-19 pandemic crisis and the difficulties of proving health products have accentuated this

48 We refer here, on the one hand, to the report of the mission chaired by the deputy Bothorel, in charge in June 2020, which was entrusted with the task of initiating a reflection on the organization of accessibility, modes of exploitation and governance of data of public interest, and, on the other hand, to the European strategy underway to facilitate the sharing and use of data in the public and private sectors.

49 This imperative of sovereignty is mentioned both by representatives of the State and representatives of private organizations in the health sector and by representatives of health professionals. We can cite, in particular, the analyses and recommendations of the *Conseil national de l'Ordre des médecins* (National Council of the Order of Physicians) published in January 2018, which state on p. 61: "The location of these infrastructures and platforms, their operation, their purposes and their regulation represent a major issue of sovereignty so that, in the future, France and Europe are not subjugated by supranational digital giants."

imperative, as evidenced by the rider to the contract signed in 2021. Health data imperative of sovereignty is fed by health data in two ways:

– On the one hand, "health sovereignty", in that they constitute the main resource from which the most innovative care for French citizens would be produced via the exploitation and enrichment of the databases held on the territory.

Key themes	Targeted measures
1) Faster access to innovation for patients. 2) Research, training: public and private, together to meet the challenges of tomorrow. 3) Mobilizing the sectors to prepare the future. 4) A more stable and predictable dialogue.	Measure 8 "Supporting companies and their employees in the digital transformation". Measure 9 "Structuring the health data ecosystem in France by creating the Health Data Hub, one of the largest health databases in the world". The methodologies that make these analyses robust are therefore crucial, and this requires four complementary levers that this measure aims to activate simultaneously: 1) facilitating the creation of increasingly rich databases that cover all aspects of the patient's care pathway: creating the conditions for interoperability, matching existing data, enriching the National Health Data System and encouraging professionals to produce new quality data; 2) facilitating the obtainment of authorizations for the processing of such data by implementing simplified procedures for the most frequent uses and by harmonizing the various procedures, while respecting the rights of individuals; 3) creating the conditions for the use of the results of the data analysis by developing the use of the data in real conditions; 4) mobilizing research communities from both health and artificial intelligence, industry and start-ups to develop new analysis methodologies, based on a "Big Data" health data infrastructure linked to the structuring of scientific cohorts and the 4) mobilizing research communities from health and artificial intelligence, industry and start-ups to develop new analysis methodologies, based on a "Big Data" health data infrastructure linked to the structuring of scientific cohorts and the France 2025 genomic medicine plan.

Table 2.5. *Measures in the 8th edition –*
May–July 2018 (É. Philippe government)

Key themes	Targeted measures
1) Strengthening our biomedical research capacity. 2) Investing in three priority areas. 3) Making France the leading country in Europe on clinical trials. 4) Enabling equity of access to care for patients and provide an accelerated and simplified market access framework for innovations. 5) Providing a predictable economic framework consistent with the objective of health and industrial sovereignty. 6) Supporting the industrialization of healthcare products in France and support the growth of companies in the sector. 7) Creating a structure to drive and strategically manage innovation in health.	Digital health is one of the three priority areas of the Health Innovation Plan 2030 (*Plan Innovation Santé 2030*), with a dedicated investment of €650 million.

Table 2.6. *Measurements during the 9th edition – June 2021 (J. Castex government)*

– On the other hand, an "industrial sovereignty" in that they would require the consolidation of a dedicated sector (skills in data processing and analysis) in order to be developed and, as such, they would be generative of employment[50]. Otherwise, the risk is that foreign players (particularly the Internet giants) will develop "algorithmic medicine tools [that do not guarantee] the ethical principle and in particular the methods of obtaining consent for data collection"[51]. In this respect, it is interesting to note that the predominance of this economic dimension is systematically accompanied by a plea for a relaxation of the legal and regulatory constraints on access to personal data.

---

50 For more details, we refer the reader to the industry contract signed in 2019 as well as its amendment in 2021.

51 Remarks by David Gruson, member of the Steering Committee of the Health Chair of the *Institut d'études politiques de Paris*, founder of Ethik-IA, interviewed during the public hearing lique conducted by the *Office parlementaire d'évaluation des choix scientifiques et technologiques sur l'intelligence artificielle et les données de santé*. Source: Report No. 401 (2018–2019) by Gérard Longuet, senator, and Cédric Villani, deputy, filed on March 21, 2019, p. 22.

In addition to the work carried out within the CSIS, a number of initiatives taken by different action plans have consolidated the anchoring of health data in the economic field:

– Digital health has been identified by a college of experts[52] as one of the priority areas of the Productive Pact announced by Emmanuel Macron in April 2019, an interministerial action program (Ministry of Economy and Finance, Ministry of Higher Education, Research and Innovation). In particular, it is mentioned that "it is essential in response to be able to impose our standards, in terms of data generation and management, on which the development of these digital solutions drastically depends"[53].

– The digital roadmap implemented as part of the *Ma Santé 2022* plan, launched in April 2019 by the Ministry of Health, has resulted in the reactivation of the *Conseil du numérique en santé* (CNS). This body, composed of "health representatives of the various stakeholders of e-health in France, institutional, public and private"[54] has set up a working group on "Economic development of digital health" from March 2020, which "has gradually focused on structuring the digital health sector"[55]. This working group[56] was co-directed by Robert Picard, health referent of the Conseil général de l'économie at the French Ministry of the Economy and Finance, and Nicole Hill, international director of the healthcare sector at Alcatel-Lucent Enterprise. In a report, delivered in June 2021, "the controlled circulation of data in the service of AI and research" is identified as one of three major lines of action. In particular, it is recommended to "accelerate access to data; strengthen collaboration with the support of the public authorities around data between data-producing healthcare providers and industrial players"[57].

– The roadmap of the Ministry of Health and Solidarity established in September 2021 as part of the public policy on data, algorithms and code-sources launched in the wake of the Bothorel report, clearly mentions

---

52 This college of experts is chaired by the CEO of Air Liquide, and is made up of qualified personalities who are members of the Innovation Council, as well as various representatives of public institutions and other organizations.

53 Source: Collège d'experts, 2020, p. 36.

54 Action 2 of the Roadmap: Accelerating the digital shift.

55 Source: Picard and Hill, 2021, p. 3.

56 This working group is composed of 35 people, mostly from the private sector.

57 Source: Picard and Hill 2020, p. 12.

that "fostering the creation of economic value and offering resources for innovation" is a key issue.

– The predominance of economic issues is also reflected in the close cooperation between representatives of private economic interests and representatives of public bodies within the various bodies responsible for drawing up the contours of health data policy in France. For example, the creation of the health data exploitation platform (HDH) announced by Emmanuel Macron in March 2018 was preceded by the establishment of a working group by the ministry of Health, aiming to "propose a roadmap for the next four years relating to the reconciliation of clinical data and medico-administrative data from the SNDS"[58] and to "propose an organization for this alliance as well as the definition of the data platform and the service offering it would provide and how it would facilitate the development of the ecosystem (public players, research, start-ups and other private actors...)"[59]. This prefiguration mission of the HDH was co-directed[60] by Dominique Polton, president of the INDS, Marc Cuggia, a hospital practitioner and "specialist in hospital repositories"[61], and Gilles Wainrib, president and founder of the start-up Owkin, "a recognized start-up in the field of healthcare data"[62].

We can therefore clearly see a shift from regulation to data access in France, through the choice of co-regulation between public and private actors, and the establishment of a centralized public structure for health data (HDH). However, while these decisions appear iconoclastic in several

---

58 Source: draft engagement letter memo to the Minister of Health from the Director of DREES, May 4, 2018.

59 Source: mission letter to INDS President, Pr Marc Cuggia, and Gilles Wainrib, May 16, 2018.

60 It is also composed of 14 members: three representatives of research organizations (CNRS, Inria and Inserm), three representatives of the health administration (DREES and *Délégation à la stratégie des systèmes d'information en santé* – DSSIS), a representative of the *Direction générale de la recherche et de l'innovation* (DGRI) and a representative of the *Direction interministérielle du numérique et du système d'information et de communication de l'État* (DINSIC), a representative of the health insurance fund, a representative of a healthcare institution and a hospital practitioner, a representative of the French Pharmaceutical Companies Union (LEEM) and two representatives of start-ups in the field.

61 Source: draft engagement letter memo to the Minister of Health from the Director of DREES, May 4, 2018.

62 Source: draft engagement letter memo to the Minister of Health from the Director of DREES, May 4, 2018.

respects, they are part of a series of reforms undertaken from the 2010s onwards, which have seen access to health data become a problem of general interest (Aubry 2016). However, while this representation of access to data is widely supported, transcending public–private divides, the recent ruling on the structuring of the HDH reveals the historical conflictual dimension attached to the issue of regulation of health data in France.

Announced by Emmanuel Macron in March 2018, this health data platform is presented as a central element of French policy to support the development of artificial intelligence. It must respond to the many criticisms concerning access to and secondary use of existing health databases (dispersion of data, long and complex access times).

Scheduled by the law of July 24, 2019 on the organization and transformation of the healthcare system, this new structure was officially created on November 30, 2019 as a public interest group. As the CNIL points out[63], the term "health data hub" (or HDH) refer simultaneously to: the public interest group responsible for setting up and administering this platform, which succeeded the *Institut des données de santé* (INDS); to the technical solution: a technological platform that allows data to be stored and made available.

This platform integrates in its scope of action the SNDS databases as well as "data from registers, research cohorts, hospital data, town medicine, etc." (Combes et al. 2020). Its mission is to facilitate the sharing of health data from a wide variety of sources, "with the aim of improving the quality of care and patient support. In concrete terms, it centralizes non-identifying data hosted on a secure platform, in compliance with regulations and citizens' rights"[64]. This structure translates into a "one-stop shop for access requests and [the provision of] powerful, high-level computing resources to facilitate the analysis of very large datasets using space- and computationally-intensive methods" (Goldberg and Zins 2021). A representative of the DGE was present, as well as representatives from the economic world (LEEM, the *Association française des entreprises de la recherche clinique*, the *Syndicat national de l'industrie des technologies médicales*, etc.) within its governance, which involves nearly 56 stakeholders.

Box 2.3. *The health data hub*

---

63 Source: CNIL website: https://www.cnil.fr/fr/la-plateforme-des-donnees-de-sante-health-data-hub [Accessed on July 03, 2022].
64 Source: https://www.health-data-hub.fr/faq-en-francais [Accessed July 03, 2022].

2.3. A contested regulatory vision

The successive initiatives taken since the mid-2010s show that the issue of health data regulation in France is particularly delicate. While public health databases are unanimously considered a national "treasure"[65] and constitute a "common heritage" (Combes et al. 2020), the way in which they are made accessible, although recognized as a major issue, is the subject of much controversy.

While the State is now positioning itself as a facilitator of the health data ecosystem (under the title of "metaplatform State", a concept defended by the ministerial delegation for digital technology)[66], it has long been uninterested in the subject, thus working to create a form of opacity around access to databases, a consequence of a complex health system (see section 2.3.1). The political agenda set in recent years, far from simplifying the contours, has contributed to reinforcing the conflictual dimension under the effect of interministerial rivalries (see section 2.3.2), and of a restrictive vision of the involvement of health professionals (see section 2.3.3).

2.3.1. *A complex health system*

In view of the new health and economic purposes that health data will increasingly serve, successive governments will strategically reposition themselves in the governance of data (Aubry 2016).

This is reflected, on the one hand, in the central role assumed, as of the end of 2015, by DREES (a department under the joint supervision of the Ministry of Health and the Ministry of the Economy and Finance, among others) in "the governance of health data and the definition of the rules for

---

65 Expression used by D. Sicard and J.M. Spaeth in an article entitled "Il faut 'ouvrir les données publiques de santé à tous les acteurs'", published on September 27, 2016 in *Le Monde*.
66 Source: https://www.hospimedia.fr/actualite/articles/20190411-e-sante-le-numerique-en-sante-doit-evoluer [Accessed March 7, 2022]. This "(consists) of the public authorities defining the general framework for the urbanization of health information systems and guaranteeing its ethics, while leaving the development of value-added services to private players" (TicPharma, March 29, 2019).

making them available [...]"[67]; and, on the other hand, by taking into account the criticisms formulated concerning the opening and exploitation of health data from medico-administrative databases. Thus, following the report[68] submitted by Pierre-Louis Bras, Inspector General of Social Affairs, the Ministry of Health and Social Affairs drew up the law on the modernization of the health system adopted on January 26, 2016, creating the SNDS. This legislation is intended to provide a response to the difficulties of steering the SNIIram, which is split between the *Comité d'orientation et de pilotage de l'information interrégimes* (Copiir), the *Institut des données de santé* (IDS) and the *Caisse nationale de l'assurance maladie des travailleurs salariés* (CNAMTS) (since 2018, the *Caisse nationale de l'assurance maladie*, Cnam). The creation of the SNDS is accompanied by a distinction between strategic, technical and operational functions[69]. Specifically, the CNAMTS "will ensure the day-to-day operation of the system and its development, in accordance with the guidelines set by the strategic committee on the basis of the needs expressed within the INDS"[70]. This new organization aims to "increase the number of users of medico-administrative data, harmonize access procedures and shorten delays, improve data security and facilitate matching"[71].

However, as indicated in the previous section, this new configuration does not put an end to the discontent of professionals both public and private sectors. While everyone agrees that the State has clarified its doctrine[72], the regulation of access by the type of data (re-identifiable or not) is not very appropriate for applications in artificial intelligence. Similarly, although the procedures have been simplified for actors operating in the public sector, they remain tedious for other actors despite the implementation of a

---

67 Quoted in the report of the Cour des Comptes, Les données personnelles de santé gérées par l'Assurance maladie. Une utilisation à développer, une sécurité à renforcer, March 2016, p. 94.

68 This report, submitted in September 2013, consists of a series of proposals to set up a system for accessing and using medico-administrative databases. Note that the content of this report is an integral part of the decisions taken at the end of the 6e edition of the CSIS in July 2013.

69 Source: Cour des Comptes, 2016, pp. 93–96.

70 Source: Cour des Comptes, 2016, p. 95.

71 Source: Franck von Lennep, DREES, Les Ateliers de Giens, March 29, 2017.

72 Source: Open Data Commission, 2014, p. 26.

reference methodology and the INDS (Aubry 2016). Finally, the proposed organization remains fragmented in the absence of harmonization of the governance of existing databases[73]. The national policy in the field of health data is thus strongly marked by the silostructure of the French health system (Pierru and Rolland 2016, p. 488): "regulation (mainly the State), financing (Social Security and supplementary health insurance), and the 'production' of care (general medicine, hospitals, and medical-social services)". In concrete terms, this translates into a far from obvious coordination between the central administrations, each of which is competent in their respective fields of action: the *Direction générale de l'organisation des soins* (DGOS) on hospital data via the *Agence technique de l'information sur l'hospitalisation* (ATIH) and the PMSI, the *Direction de la sécurité sociale sur les données de l'assurance maladie*, and the *Direction générale de la cohésion sociale* (DGCS) via the *Caisse nationale de solidarité pour l'autonomie* (CNSA) on medico-social data[74].

These cooperation difficulties are coupled with a lack of convergence within the health administration of Big Data processing. Indeed, following interviews with representatives of the former *Délégation à la stratégie des systèmes d'information en santé* (DSSIS)[75], two competing visions can be observed: on the one hand, support for strategies that would consist of encouraging the development of algorithms on the basis of existing data, without coding, i.e. without a process of structuring the data in advance. On the other hand, reference is made to what is happening in the field of shared medical records, of the communicating file in oncology, where the aim is to carry out a process of standardization of practices (via, for example, the development of common structured reports) in order to then resort to AI.

However, this issue seems to have been recently resolved by the new ministerial delegation for digital health (DNS) created in 2019, which lists among its priority actions the "implementation of a health terminology management center (*centre de gestion des terminologies de santé*, CGTS) with multi terminologies (*serveur multiterminologies*, SMT) server to

---

73 Source: Cour des comptes, 2016, p. 94.
74 Source: Cour des comptes, 2016, p. 94.
75 As of December 21, 2019, DSSIS was pulled into the *Délégation ministérielle au numérique en santé* (DNS).

support the semantic structuring of health data"[76]. More generally, the stated objective of this new structure, which reports directly to the Minister of Health, is to strengthen and clarify the governance of digital health by absorbing part of the DSSIS and the Delegation to the public health information service (*Délégation au service public d'information en santé*, SPIS), and by ensuring the management of the Digital Health Agency (*Agence du numérique en santé*, ANS, formerly ASIP) in charge of the operational implementation of the digital health policy. Although this new configuration has been widely supported[77], it does not put an end to possible difficulties in cooperation between central administrations (including the DNS) and/or between the State and the Health Insurance. This is evidenced by the recent clashes over the HDH and the solution for hosting and using health data chosen[78]. The choice of a centralized technological structure hosted in a foreign cloud has given rise to numerous criticisms from the CNIL and various associative groups (InterHop, etc.), leading the management of the HDH, in agreement with the Ministry of Health, to temporarily withdraw its request for authorization from the CNIL to host the main SNDS database and new databases. Following the reservations expressed by the CNIL in 2020, Cnam opposed the transfer of a copy of the SNDS to the hosting solution, leading it to officially refuse to contribute to the financing of the HDH for 2022.

2.3.2. *Interministerial rivalries*

Beyond the scope of the Ministry of Health alone, there are obstacles relating to the cross-cutting dimension of health data policy which is more broadly part of the field of innovation policies. This is reflected in a pile of initiatives leading to a lack of legibility of public action, even though this is systematically presented as a primary objective by the public authorities.

---

76 Source: action 10, briefing packet, feuille de route: Accélérer le virage numérique, April 25, 2019, p. 17.

77 Source: https://www.ticsante.com/story/4591/e-sante-la-feuille-de-route-ministerielle-saluee-malgre-des-interrogations-sur-le-financement.html [Accessed March 9, 2022].

78 The choice of entrusting the hosting and operation of health data to a Microsoft subsidiary has been criticized because of the Cloud Act, a law that allows the American justice system to access data stored on servers located outside the United States.

Key dates	Decisions	Objectives
November 24, 2015	Launch of the "Medicine of the Future" program	Merging of the "Digital Health" plan with the other health plans of France's reindustrialization program "New Industrial France" Establishment of a roadmap to identify an organization, promising projects and obstacles to innovation in health.
January 25, 2016	Appointment of a delegate to Health Innovation	Creating an "identified interlocutor" so that exchanges between public authorities and "innovation actors" are "simple, fast and fluid".
April 22, 2016	Launch of an online consultation on Big Data in health	Analyzing the perception of Big Data in health and collect the opinion of Internet users on the conditions in which "the public authorities should support its development".
July 4, 2016	Presentation of the strategy "e-health 2020"	– Creation of a strategic committee on digital health (CSNS). – Creation of a health data administrator function.
March 25, 2018	Launch of the AI for humanity plan	– Announcement of the creation of the HDH. – "Health" identified as a priority area for action.
April 25, 2019	Presentation of the roadmap for the "Digital Shift" project as part of the Ma Santé 2022 plan	– Announcement creation of DNS, ANS. – Replacement of CSNS with the Digital Health Council (Conseil du numérique en santé, CNS).
July 21, 2020	Presentation of "Ségur de la Santé"	Investment plan for the digital component.
January 08, 2021	"Digital health", identified as an acceleration strategy within the framework of the stimulus plan and the PIA4	– "Development of knowledge useful for the digital health of the future of the future". – "Supporting and facilitating market access". – "Development of a major French digital health ecosystem". – "Building trust in e-health through training". – "Strengthening the policy of pooling and exploiting health data".
June 29, 2021	Health Innovation Plan 2030	– "Digital health" identified as a priority area. – Creation of a health innovation agency.

Table 2.7. *Departmental health initiatives*

Inter-ministerial rivalries, particularly between the Ministry of Health, on the one hand, and the Ministry of the Economy and Finance, on the other, have doubled this lack of legibility. This lack of clarity had been evident since the implementation of the three "health plans" of the reindustrialization program launched in September 2013. Indeed, the interministerial governance of the three projects quickly proved to be delicate, with "difficulties in associating the Ministry of Health"[79] being mentioned. In April 2015, Mireille Faugères, one of the co-leaders of the "Digital Health" plan, regretted the lack of a "conductor"[80], due to the lack of identified contacts within each of the two ministries, as well as the lack of a single forum for discussion with manufacturers. The reorganization of the system by merging the three "health" plans into a new program entitled "*Solution médecine du futur*" in May 2015 jointly managed by Pr André Syrota and Olivier Charmeil, Executive Vice President of Sanofi Pasteur, will only partially put an end to the difficulties of interministerial governance. This is evidenced by the appointment by the Minister of Health, on January 25, 2016, of a delegate for innovation in health. Admittedly, the identification of a privileged "interlocutor" within the Ministry of Health is a response to the shortcomings previously mentioned. However, as soon as he took office, he regretted the scope of his delegation and the lack of exchanges between the Ministry of Health and the Ministry of the Economy, Finance and the Digital Economy[81]. This delegation will be abolished by the new Minister of Health, Agnès Buzyn, in December 2018.

---

79 Source: https://www.apmnews.com/freestory/10/261189/les-trois-plans-sante-de-la-nouvelle-france-industrielle-fusionnes-en-un-plan-medecine-du-futur [Accessed November 15, 2021].

80 Source: https://www.apmnews.com/nostory.php?uid=10&objet=260129 [Accessed November 15, 2021].

81 Source: https://www.ticpharma.com/story/133/jean-yves-fagon-veut-faire-le-tri-dans-les-innovations-en-sante-en-redefinissant-l-evaluation.html [Accessed November 15, 2021]. "The key issue is, 'Are these two structures capable of exchanging?' 'That was very, very little when I arrived. Now we are starting to have real debates,' Jean-Yves Fagon assured. 'I considered that Bercy was a priority, so I discussed with Bercy,' said the ministerial delegate, who also said he had spoken with the ministry in charge of research. 'It's not very simple either because everyone is also in their power and perimeter meter stakes, all of which is legitimate.'"

Subsequently, the predominance of the economic goals attached to health data led to the creation of an "interministerial task force"[82] within the framework of the Productive Pact, bringing together the Ministry of the Economy, Finance and Recovery, the Ministry of Health and Solidarity, the Ministry of Research and Innovation, and the General Secretariat for Investment. The linkage of this interministerial working group, whose secretariat is provided by the *Direction générale des entreprises* (DGE), with the actions carried out by or under the authority of the DNS is a preoccupation of the authorities, as evidenced by various reports or press kits[83], or even an appointment[84]. It is also embodied in the investment of Robert Picard, the "health" referent the Ministry of the Economy and Finance, both as the editor of the report "*Mobilisation globale dans le cadre de la stratégie d'accélération de la santé numérique*"[85] and as co-leader of the working group "Structuring the digital health sector" within the CNS. In short, the interministerial dimension is taking shape in the form of public action clearly geared towards the exploitation and economic development of health data.

2.3.3. *A professional sector under tension*

This orientation is also in tune with health professionals, at two levels. Firstly, the mode of elaboration of public decisions in the field alters a little more the historical proximity between health professionals and political personnel (Hassenteufel 1997), already undermined by the emergence of a reforming administrative elite (among others, Genieys and Hassenteufel 2012). Concretely, since the overhaul of the right of access to medico-administrative databases in 2016, health professionals and their representative bodies and/or trade unions are no longer integrated in a

---

82 Source: Mission letter from the Minister for Industry to the Vice President of the General Economic Council, November 1, 2021.

83 Mission letter from the Minister for Industry to the Vice President of the General Economic Council, November 1, 2021. Report on the structuring of the digital health sector. Final report of June 18, 2021.

84 We refer here to the appointment of O. Clatz as head of the digital component of the Ségur de la santémember of the DNS, and former director of the company Therapixel; or that of David Sainati, founder of a digital health start-up and member of the DNS, in charge of supervising the "health" acceleration strategy under the authority of the under the authority of the General Secretariat for Investment.

85 Report transmitted in April 2021 upon request of the Minister for Industry.

privileged way into the functioning of the bodies in charge of regulation, health data policies or more broadly digital health regulation. This arouses great dissatisfaction on their part (Aubry 2016), insofar as not only the proposed use of medico-administrative databases can potentially work towards the development of decision support indicators in terms of surveillance of the practices of health professionals, but confines them strictly to the user side in the new system. This trend will be confirmed by the following public intervention programs. Secondly, the initiatives undertaken by health professionals themselves (e.g. the national "Impulsion ACP 2020" project, which consists of a digital network for sharing data in anatomo-cyto-pathology (ACP)) without being put is not officially supported by the public authorities, as evidenced by the obstacles encountered by its promoters in financing such a project.

In short, the main actions aimed at health professionals can be summed up as training in the uses and practices of digital tools, connected objects and artificial intelligence; raising awareness of the quality of the data produced insofar as the networking and integration of the various databases (clinical, genomic, real-life data, etc.) requires the digitization of the main sources of information (patient files, doctors' reports, etc.), as well as the definition and introduction of quality standards in data production. Although being at the heart of this production process, health professionals are – at best – reduced to this role of data provider, as we have seen in the ACP sector. This seems paradoxical, to say the least, insofar as the work of structuring data – an essential prerequisite for their exploitation – requires broad consultation between health professionals, software publishers and computer scientists. In addition, the tools developed from AI rarely meet the expectations of professionals. For example, in the case of ACP, diagnostic assistance tools are not implemented to help identify more delicate diagnostic cases, but rather for cases that do not pose any particular difficulty.

No doubt this weak association stems from the dominant conception of the expected benefits of the development of artificial intelligence in the health sector. Indeed, whatever the orientation of precision medicine (5Ps: personalized, preventive, participatory, predictive, pertinent) chosen, physicians' professional practices would be irrevocably transformed. They would have to use probabilistic data, the interpretation of which they would not be able to control. This requires a set of statistical techniques and tools that are not within the competence of physicians. Indeed, PM, by multiplying patient data and the use of complex technologies, requires the involvement of experts capable of producing and interpreting them. The intervention of third-party scientists (among others bioinformaticians, biology engineers, biologists) in the doctor–patient dialogue would be decisive for genetic and biological analyses, which go far beyond classical biological analyses.

In other words, the rise of technologies and the colossal increase in the volume of information accompanying the rise of PM would tend to call into question the central role and hierarchical domination of the doctor in the care system. In addition to the fact that the first works focusing on the effects of artificial intelligence in medical practice tend to relativize the transformations induced (Anichini and Geffroy 2021), the initiatives undertaken come up against strong institutional constraints. These are particularly linked to the persistence of a dichotomic structuring of the French biomedical landscape which hinders collaboration between medicine and experimental sciences (Vézian 2014), and result in the permanent difficulty of reconciling from a point of view regulatory view, public health needs, ethical and health risks, and economic considerations (among others, Degrassat-Théas and Bocquet 2016). More broadly, the call from the public authorities to make a massive commitment to the production and use of health data has led the players in the health system (hospital establishments as well as liberal groups) to commit individually to the economic valuation of these goods, in fact contravening the objective of mutualization on a national scale.

2.4. Conclusion

The technological changes introduced at the turn of the 21st century have had a major impact on the digitization capacities of existing data, on the production of new data both within and outside the health field (mobile applications, etc.), as well as on their processing in terms of analysis and storage, contributing to a renewed interest in data applied to the health field. The Open Data movement undertaken on an international scale during the 2000s has led to a shift in the issue of health data regulation to the field of economics and innovation. The placing of digital health on the agenda of successive governments has made a significant contribution to the structuring of a genuine medical data policy in France in all its dimensions, as shown by the many initiatives mentioned. However, if these impulses have proved decisive in overhauling the organizational architecture for the production and use of health data, the fact remains that they are largely dependent on political will. Positioned as a central issue in health policies and, more generally, as a key lever for economic development in a context of global competition, digital technology has become a strong political force. The absence of references to previous policies in successive e-health strategies is proof of this. Of course, it would be hard to imagine that this sector would be neglected by public authorities, particularly in light of the lessons learned about the importance of digital technology in the management of the Covid-19 pandemic (Agence numérique de santé 2020). On the other hand, the socio-economic issues raised by this same pandemic (increased inequalities in access to care, human resources available to healthcare institutions, etc.) could potentially lead public authorities to focus on other priority themes, relegating the status of digital technology to that of a simple tool for dealing with these inequalities, rather than being considered as a specific issue. As a result, the considerable resources allocated to support the missions entrusted to the Agence numérique de santé (recruitment of nearly 30 people in 2020, including five dedicated to the implementation of the agency's policy, for a total of 170 employees, i.e. 67% more than in 2019)[86], but more broadly, the mode of governance set up for this digital strategy would be called into question (in particular, the sustainability of the DNS, the proclaimed spearhead of an integrating strategy).

2.5. References

Agence numérique en santé (2021). Rapport d'activité 2020. Ministère des Solidarités et de la Santé, Paris.

Anichini, G. and Geffroy, B. (2021). L'intelligence artificielle à l'épreuve des savoirs tacites. Analyse des pratiques d'utilisation d'un outil d'aide à la détection en radiologie. *Sciences sociales et santé*, 39, 43–69.

Aubry, A. (2016). La mise à l'agenda politique de l'ouverture de l'accès aux données médico-administratives du Système national d'information interrégimes de l'Assurance maladie (SNIIRAM) et l'évolution parallèle de sa gouvernance. Master's Thesis, Université Lumière Lyon 2/Institut d'Études politiques de Lyon, Lyon.

---

86 Source: Activity Report, Agence numérique de santé 2020; https://www.ticsante.com/story/5879/e-health-the-dns-and-the-sereins-before-the-presidential-election-of-2022.html [Accessed October 10, 2021].

Aubry, A. (2017). La politisation et l'évolution de la gouvernance d'accès et d'utilisation des données de santé par les assureurs complémentaires face aux nouveaux modes de production et de traitement de l'information de santé. Master's Thesis, Université Lumière Lyon 2/Institut d'Études politiques de Lyon, Lyon.

BCG, BPIFrance, BioUp, Francebiotech (2021). Plan Healthtech. Du vivier aux grandes réussites. Report, Paris.

Bernelin, M. (2019). Intelligence artificielle en santé : la ruée vers les données personnelles. *Cités*, 4(80), 75–89.

Bévière-Boyer, B. (2021). La gestion des données de santé par le Heath Data Hub : le recours à la société Microsoft, entre risques et précautions. *Droit, santé et société*, 3, 42–48.

Bothorel, E. (2021). Pour une politique publique de la donnée. Report, Paris.

Castel, P. and Vézian, A. (2018). Le gouvernement de la biomédecine par l'organisation. Le cas de la cancérologie française. In *Le cancer : un regard sociologique – Biomédicalisation et parcours de soins*, Amsellem, N. (ed.). La Découverte, Paris.

Chevallier, J. (2018). Vers l'État-plateforme ? *Revue française d'administration publique*, 3(167), 627–637.

Chevallier, J. and Cluzel-Métayer, L. (2018). Introduction. *Revue française d'administration publique*, 3(167), 463–470.

Collège d'experts (2020). Faire de la France une économie de rupture technologique. Soutenir les marchés émergents à forts enjeux de compétitivité. Report to the Ministre de l'Économie et des finances and the Ministre de l'Enseignement supérieur, de la recherche et de l'innovation, Paris.

Combes, S., Bacry, E., Fontbonne, C. (2020). Health Data Hub : plateforme des données de santé en France, application à l'oncologie radiothérapie. *Cancer/Radiothérapie*, 24(6–7), 762–767.

Commission Open data en santé (2014). Report, Ministère des Affaires sociales et de la Santé, Paris.

Cour des comptes (2016). Les données personnelles de santé gérées par l'assurance maladie. Une utilisation à développer, une sécurité à renforcer. Report, Cour des Comptes.

Dagiral, É. and Peerbaye, A. (2013). Voir pour savoir : concevoir et partager des "vues" à travers une base de données biomédicales. *Réseaux*, 2–3(178–179), 163–196.

Degrassat-Théas, A. and Bocquet, F. (2016). Les recommandations temporaires d'utilisation pour les médicaments ou comment concilier enjeux de santé publique et enjeux économiques ? *Médecine & Droit*, 137, 48–55.

Devillier, N. (2017). Les dispositions de la loi de modernisation de notre système de santé relatives aux données de santé. *Journal international de bioéthique et d'éthique des sciences*, 3(28), 57–61.

Genieys, W. and Hassenteufel, P. (2012). Qui gouverne les politiques publiques ? Par delà la sociologie des élites. *Gouvernement et action publique*, 2, 89–115.

Goldberg, M. and Zins, M. (2021). Le Health Data Hub (fin) de multiples problèmes et des solutions alternatives ? *Médecine/Science*, 37(3), 277–281.

Hassenteufel, P. (1997). *Les médecins face à l'État – Une comparaison européenne*. Presses de Sciences Po, Paris.

Leonelli, S. (2014). What difference does quantity make? On the epistemology of Big Data in biology. *Big Data & Society*, 1–11.

Picard, R. (2021). Mobilisation globale dans le cadre de la stratégie d'accélération de la santé numérique. Report to the Ministre déléguée chargée de l'Industrie, auprès and the Ministre de l'Économie, des finances et de la relance, Conseil générale de l'économie, Paris.

Picard, R. and Hill, N. (2020). Structuration de la filière en santé numérique. Report, Conseil du Numérique en Santé et Conseil général de l'économie, Paris.

Picard, R. and Hill, N. (2021). Structuration de la filière en santé numérique. Report, Conseil du Numérique en Santé et Conseil général de l'économie, Paris.

Pierru, F. and Rolland, C. (2016). Bringing the health care state back in. Les embarras politiques d'une intégration par fusion : le cas des Agences Régionales de Santé. *Revue française de science politique*, 66, 483–506.

Polton, D. (2018). Les données de santé. *Médicine/Science*, 34(5), 449–455.

Robin, A. (2021). Open data et santé : quelles modalités pour la diffusion et l'exploitation des données de santé ? *Journal international de bioéthique et d'éthique des sciences*, 2(32), 33–44.

Vézian, A. (2014). À la recherche d'une politique biomédicale en France : chronique d'une réforme inaboutie en cancérologie. *Sociologie du travail*, 56(2), 204–224.

Villani, C. (2018). Donner un sens à l'intelligence artificielle – Pour une stratégie nationale et européenne. Report, Paris.

Zins, M., Cuggia, M., Goldberg, M. (2021). Les données de santé en France : abondantes mais complexes. *Médecine/Science*, 37(2), 179–184.

3

Access Policies to Digital Resources of Administration through the Lens of Microsimulation

To tell you the little story of why we got excited about microsimulation, it's that Anthony Atkinson had a rather extraordinary experience: he was relatively close to the Labour Party [...] At the time of the budget speech in the English Parliament, the Prime Minister makes his speech and indicates all the reforms that are going to take place. Atkinson had convinced Gordon Brown that it was possible to simulate the effects of his reforms almost simultaneously with the Prime Minister's announcement [...]. The Prime Minister made his speech that day. Gordon Brown asked for a half-hour recess, during which Atkinson did his calculations on his computer, which at the time was rudimentary, and he came out with the results and said, "This is what your reform is going to do, there are so many winners, so many losers, the winners are these people, the losers are those people." The British Parliament was absolutely amazed that the opposition had been able to produce these results in such a short time. And it's a bit on this that we launched the microsimulation project, because we thought we were going to convince journalists, parliamentarians to

Chapter written by Franck BESSIS and Paul COTTON.

systematically use this product (Interview with François Bourguignon, July 2021).

This excerpt from an interview with one of the pioneers of microsimulation in France summarizes the challenge of disseminating this tool for designing and evaluating tax-benefit policies. Making microsimulation models available to a wider public (researchers, journalists, parliamentarians and even taxpayers and/or recipients of social benefits, voters) rather than restricting their use to administrations alone also implies opening up access to the data necessary for their operation. The relationship between digital tools and public action can then be considered in two complementary ways in the case of this object. On the one hand, as policy reform instruments developed thanks to the progress of computer science, microsimulation models are presented as digital tools for public action. On the other hand, the place they have taken over the last 30 years also invites us to take an interest in certain forms of public action on the digital, namely the policy of access to the administration's digital resources, the way in which actors negotiate margins of manoeuvring on the basis of these resources by seizing them, by circumventing their spirit or even by seeking to make them evolve. This public action is therefore not simply the product of political will, but is the result of a mobilization of actors from different backgrounds: INSEE officers, economic researchers and Open Data activists within or outside the administration. Based on the evolution of the microsimulation landscape in France, this chapter focuses on two issues of the policy of access to the administration's digital resources: the first concerns access to the administration's models ("Open Access", the second is the opening of its data ("Open Data")[1]. These issues result in more or less direct confrontations with the administration, aiming to promote and expand the trend reversal introduced by Open Data according to which "public data and information must be published online even before being reclaimed by third parties" (Beranger 2017), or in other words "the voluntary and proactive dissemination of data, mostly public, that become freely reusable" (Goëta 2015).

Before going into more detail about this opening-up movement, which is studied here through the prism of microsimulation, it is appropriate to briefly

---

1 Legally, a database is understood as "a collection of works, data or other independent elements, arranged in a systematic or methodical way, and individually accessible by electronic means or by any other means" (article L112-3 of July 2, 1998).

introduce this instrument. Microsimulation models can be either static, and reconstitute the impact of the policy on individuals at a given moment, or dynamic, and reconstitute this impact throughout a lifecycle of the individual (Blanchet 2015). This chapter focuses on static models, applied to the French monetary redistribution system. More specifically, it will discuss the Ines, Myriade, Openfisca, Saphir and Taxipp[2] models. These models are made up of several elements. First, they reproduce in computer code form the social and fiscal legislation in a simplified form[3]. Based on this legislation, a micro-economical database containing individual information on a representative sample of the population makes it possible to simulate the effects of the tax-benefit system in terms of redistribution and budget masses. This database can be compiled from a survey (e.g. *"Budget des familles"*, Family Budget)[4] or from the application of a survey and administrative data (e.g. tax returns and the *"Enquête Emploi"*, Employment Survey)[5]. Unlike social and fiscal legislation, which is accessible to all via the *Journal officiel*[6], these data are not freely available. Produced by the administrations themselves, some of the information they contain are subject to professional secrecy (data relating to family or personal situation, tax situation, etc.). Once these two ingredients are combined (the legal code and the micro-economic data), the microsimulation models make it possible to modify the current tax-benefit system by setting up one or more evolution scenarios. By comparing the results obtained in this way with the results obtained without any modification, the evaluation of the redistributive and budgetary impacts of the scenario(s) can be made. These models are also used to draw up the redistributive assessments that are widely reported in the press each year around the presentation of the *projet de loi de finances* (draft budget bill)[7].

---

2 For a more complete history of static microsimulation in France, see Legendre (2019) and Bessis and Cotton (2021).

3 This code can be written in different computer languages. For example, and not exhaustively: SAS, for a language that requires a paying license; C++, R, or Python for "free" languages, and therefore free.

4 https://www.insee.fr/fr/metadonnees/source/serie/s1194.

5 https://www.insee.fr/fr/metadonnees/source/serie/s1223.

6 The cost of entry for its understanding remains high, however.

7 The latest example: the redistributive balance sheet of Emmanuel Macron's five-year term produced from the Treasury's microsimulation model for the 2022 economic, social and financial report annexed to the finance bill. "Macron, président des riches. L'heure des comptes," *Libération*, October 11, 2021, pp. 1–5; "Macron cherche à effacer son image de

A first study of the opening movement of codes and data related to microsimulation has been proposed by Shulz (2019). Focusing on the process of developing Openfisca, the author concludes that successful mobilization for this openness relies on the "collaboration of public and non-public actors at the periphery of [the] administration" (Shulz 2019, p. 867). By resituating the Openfisca episode in the history of the development of static microsimulation models, we propose completing this analysis on two aspects. The first concerns the intervention of other actors located at the heart of the administration, and more precisely at the heart of the official statistics system. The second concerns the divergence of views between the actors who took part in this movement: rather than a "collaboration of actors", we tend to reveal and debate a plurality of conceptions of quality of openness, i.e. both conceptions of what is important to open and how to open well.

The preferred concept in this perspective is that of "statactivism", which refers to the set of actions carried out in a way that "puts statistics at the service of emancipation" (Bruno et al. 2014). The demands for the opening of codes and data of the administration are situated upstream of the ways of "making statistics a critical weapon" studied so far in this perspective, whether it is a matter of consolidating new categories "on which one can rely to claim rights and defend interests" (e.g. the category of "*intellos précaires*", precarious intellectuals) or "opposing alternative indicators to the institution" (such as the "new indicators of wealth"). Before "fighting with numbers", the actors whose approaches we are reporting on are fighting for access to the means of production of the institution. One of these original forms of "statactivist strategy" (the one that aims at access to data) has direct consequences on the affirmation of a collective category claimed on the signs of protesters at the turn of the 2010s with the slogan "We are the 99%". The other strategy, centered on access to the administration's economic models, aims less at an alternative definition of reality than at a transformation of the conditions of the democratic debate, by equipping the

---

'président des riches'" *Le Monde*, October 6, 2021, p. 16; "L'exécutif satisfait d'avoir augmenté le pouvoir d'achat des Français depuis 2017," *Le Figaro*, October 5, 2021, p. 22. Followed by counter-figures produced a few weeks later by the Institute for Public Policy: "Le quinquennat Macron a bien été celui des ultra-riches," *Médiapart*, November 17, 2021; "Pouvoir d'achat: l'étude qui relance le débat sur les gagnants du quinquennat," *Les Echos*, November 17, 2021, p. 2; "Pouvoir d'achat: le mandat Macron à la loupe," *Le Monde*, November 17, 2021, p. 14.

actors of this debate with new capacities of argumentation and counter-argumentation[8].

This chapter therefore aims specifically to describe how these two strategies are embodied, develop and coexist in the history of microsimulation[9]. Access to microeconomic data and access to model codes, both between administrations and outside them, constitute two very different phenomena, driven by "issue entrepreneurs" (Cobb and Elder 1972) with often distinct profiles and motivations. Beyond the question of why some actors focus on access to data rather than codes (or vice versa), this chapter will seek to assess the efficiency of the different strategies deployed to access them. The analysis is based on the overlap of two sources of empirical data. A study of the scientific literature on the subject was carried out to better identify the microsimulation ecosystem, its actors and its stakes. This use is justified by the fact that the academic literature on microsimulation has mainly been written by actors invested in the development of this practice, most of whom were met during interviews. About 40 interviews were also conducted between 2019 and 2021 with actors invested in microsimulation, mainly researchers and top civil servants, as well as a representative of the association that forced the opening of several models.

In the first section, we will present the situation that prevailed until the early 2000s. At that time, the development of microsimulation outside the administration was limited by a legislative framework that was not very favorable to the use of tax data by researchers. This framework will gradually evolve, allowing possible but not mandatory access to the data most suitable for the simulation of the tax-benefit system. In section 3.2, we will try to show why and how a movement to open up these data has

---

8 It is in this sense that we understand the anecdote reported at the beginning of this introduction. We can also mention as an example the expected effects of the production in the early 2000s of an alternative measure of the evolution of inequalities with the Barometer of Inequalities and Poverty (BIP 40): "The interest of a barometer such as the BIP 40 is not only to provide elements of observation on inequalities and poverty, but also to allow all the actors concerned to exercise their critical reflection, to debate and to act better to combat these inequalities" (Concialdi 2014, p. 211).

9 However, these two strategies are not exhaustive, since some actors are working to reuse codes and data outside the framework of the democratic debate. See in particular datactivist.coop, a worker cooperative (SCOP) founded by Samuel Goëta, among others, following his thesis work on Open Data.

emerged since the 2010s. Section 3.3 will deal with the opening of the codes of the administration, which closely follows that of the data. Finally, section 3.4 will be an opportunity to confront the conceptions of the quality of openness of codes and data defended by the different actors of our history.

3.1. From a circumvented closure to a progressive and non-systematic opening of data (1951–2001)

The history of the opening of French data of the administration and their conditions of access[10] has been widely documented, particularly with regard to statistical and survey databases (Rhein 2002; Chenu, Silberman 2011; Caporali et al. 2015). The development of microsimulation is fully in line with this history, with some specificities that we focus on next in order to better grasp the soil in which the double movement of opening (of codes and data) was subsequently created.

3.1.1. Outside of the administration, researchers who manage to access data in an "informal" way

The first microsimulation experiments were conducted in France at the end of the 1960s by the Direction de la prévision. Academics followed suit a few years later, with the Sysiff model developed in the 1980s within the Delta laboratory (EHESS). While it is understandable that the question of access to the microeconomic data necessary for the operation of their model did not present any difficulty at the time for the Forecasting Department, it did however arise for the teams in the Delta. And for good reason, at that time, the main legal framework of reference for researchers was that established by the 1951 law on statistical confidentiality statistical confidentiality[11]. As a result, databases containing information on the personal, family or private situation of individuals cannot be communicated outside the administration, even for research purposes. These data are

---

10 The legislative provisions allowing and framing access to data are grouped within the Code of relations between the public and the administration, which came into force on January 1, 2016, in the continuity of the "simplification shock" desired by President François Hollande.

11 Law no. 51-711 of June 7, 1951 on the obligation, the coordination and the secrecy in the field of statistics.

considered confidential and must not be circulated. In other words, researchers cannot request access to any of the administration's survey data. The spirit of this law is in fact primarily to ensure "the sealing between the services of the State" to protect and maintain the confidence of the people solicited for these surveys, by guaranteeing that their information (i.e. their data) will only be used for statistical purposes – and not, for example, to check whether they have filled out their tax return correctly (Silberman 2011). A legislative change occurred in 1978[12]. The latter allows citizens (and therefore researchers) to request access to any administrative document (including statistical data), provided that the latter are not nominative or indirectly nominative[13]. Access to administrative survey data on request is therefore theoretically possible. However, this is not access by default. The administration can refuse access on a number of grounds, such as "a secret protected by law" (article 6 of the law of 1978). In this case, the applicant must refer the matter to the newly created *Commission d'accès aux documents administratifs*, Cada[14], which must then formulate an opinion on whether or not the refusal is justified. The applicant must then negotiate access to the administrative document again, and if it is refused again, they must take the matter to the *tribunal administrative* (administrative court).

While we might expect the teams working on the development of the Sysiff model to attempt to access survey data of the administration based on the 1978 law, these researchers used data obtained in two other ways. The first appears to be[15] reuse of a source made available for a previous research contract. For its first version, Sysiff used an INSEE database – the *Enquête revenus fiscaux* (ERF, Tax Income Survey) – to which its designers had had access thanks to research conducted for the *Caisse nationale des allocations familiales* (Cnaf). This practice was not considered problematic because it was not visible, as long as the researchers did not advertise it[16]. The second

---

12 Law no. 78-17 of January 6, 1978 relating to data processing, files and freedoms.

13 This expression refers to the possibility of identifying people from a combination of variables.

14 French Commission for Access to Administrative Documents.

15 This first element was not directly confirmed by the respondents concerned, who could not remember the exact conditions under which they had had access to the ERF, although they admitted that this interpretation was likely, since the report for Cnaf did mention the use of the ERF shortly before the creation of Sysiff.

16 Another reuse of the Sysiff-independent ERF has been published in an academic journal.

way of accessing data is through direct, unofficial transmission. At the time, the dissemination of data was tacitly left to the discretion of the people who had access to them within the administration: either directly from the people in charge of the surveys, or from the people who use these databases for statistical purposes, or from people at a higher hierarchical level. In this way, the creators of the Sysiff model had access to data from another INSEE survey (Budget des familles). This transmission involved anonymization work to ensure that the data transmitted were not directly or indirectly nominative. And again, this practice did not create any difficulty as long as it remained discreet:

> At the time, relatively few researchers were working with microeconomic data because it was not available. I did some work in Syldavia[17] on micro-economic databases and I must say that I simply stole the databases in question, smuggled them out of Syldavia [...] I came back with these huge tapes of computers that made people dream at the time, they said "here is this, it is the year 2000". I came out of Syldavia with three or four tapes of this type under my arm. One day in Paris, I went to see the director of INSEE at the time [...] and I asked him, "How is it that researchers in France do not have the possibility of using these microeconomic data?" And very discreetly, he had me give him the Family Budget survey, again practically on the sly, telling me "We'll give it to you, we'll anonymize it a little more, but don't talk about it too much" [...]. Nor did he want to make an open and public commitment to say 'from now on, we're going to make this data available to the public' (Interview with François Bourguignon, July 2021).

The general observation made by Caporali et al. (2015, p. 575) is illustrated here by the early phases of the history of micro simulation: "No right of access for university researchers to data produced by the official statistical service was provided for in the agreements with the CNRS and INSEE, which led some of them to rely on personal contacts within INSEE or other administrations" (Ibid., p. 575).

---

17 The name of the country has been changed.

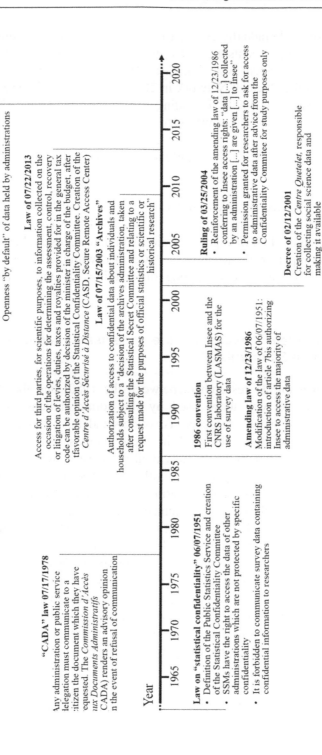

Figure 3.1. *Major steps in opening up jurisdictional data in the history of microsimulation. Authors' reconstruction*

The situation will gradually evolve towards more formal relations, via the establishment of agreements between the CNRS and INSEE (Silberman 2011). The first agreement was signed in 1986, and was renewed until the establishment of the Quetelet Network in 2001. The latter will be responsible for making social science data (including survey data from the 1970s to the 1990s) available to researchers, provided that their use is limited to research purposes and under the condition that the files are anonymized (i.e. without certain data that would make it possible to indirectly reconstruct the identity of the respondents).

These ways of accessing data, however, pose several limitations for the development of microsimulation models outside of government. Although they were among the first to engage in microsimulation, researchers have not been able to compete with the models developed within it (Ines, Myriade, then Saphir). This gap is due, among other things, to the nature of the available data.

3.1.2.   *Incomplete   access: the   decisive   advantage   of "Administrative Economists"*

The data available to researchers between the 1980s and the 2000s are difficult to compete with those used by the administrations involved in microsimulation, in several respects. To understand this, it is necessary to clarify the nature of the data used in these models. As a reminder, a microsimulation model requires an individual database on which to apply the different scenarios to be compared. Several types of sources have been used during the various microsimulation experiments in France: (1) survey data such as the Family Budget Survey; (2) administrative data: data from tax returns, sampled such as the sampled income tax file (Felin) or exhaustive such as the Pote file; (3) matching between survey data and administrative data: The Tax Income Survey (ERF) is the result of a matching of employment survey data with the tax returns file. These sources, produced by different administrations, contain their own data and therefore allow for more or less precise simulations (on more or less aspects, more or less individuals or households). In general, three criteria can be used to assess their relative quality. First, the sampling ratios applied according to the categories of population that we wish to examine in greater detail (exhaustivity of the top quintile of income distribution having even become an issue of primary importance for microsimulators over the last two decades). Second, their periodicity: is the database updated at regular intervals, every year (as is the case today for the ERF), every two years, every four years (the former periodicity of the ERF before 1996)? Are the models based on the latest vintage, or on a dated version? Finally, their nature: are they survey data or administrative data. Thus, not all data are equal.

This being the case, we understand the inherent limitations of the ways of accessing the databases that prevailed until the early 2000s. As Legendre (2019) points out, "there can be no microsimulation model without a sufficiently reliable representative sample", i.e. one that is close to the criteria of quality criteria mentioned above. In the early 2000s, Sysiff used the Family Budget source based on survey data. Another model developed by researchers at the University of Cergy in collaboration with the *Observatoire français des conjonctures économiques* (OFCE) in the early 2000s, on the other hand, benefits from more recent vintages (ERF 1998, Budget des familles 2000 and 2001, obtained thanks to a contract with Parliament for the development of the model). While it can for a time play on the same level as the models of the administration (and in particular that of INSEE, which also uses ERF for its microsimulation model Ines), the failure to update the[18] databases will contribute to making the model less and less able to produce results adapted to the current year. Moreover, having a better database is not enough to produce a better model, since the integration of a new database that is not a simple update of the previous one requires work to (re)develop the model. Even if the researchers had had access to these data outside the administration, development work would have had to be undertaken to integrate these changes into the models in question.

This issue of access to data also concerns, to a lesser extent, the various units of the official statistical service (*Service de statistiques public* SSP, composed of the ministerial statistical services[19] and INSEE) involved in

18 Since 1996, the Tax Income Survey has been updated annually, as opposed to five years ago. New versions are thus produced every year.

19 The annex to decree no. 2009-250 of March 3, 2009, on the *Autorité de la statistique publique*, updated by order on September 11, 2020, defines 16 ministerial statistical services, spread across all ministerial fields. For example, it includes the *Direction de l'animation de la recherche, des études et des statistiques* (Dares) on the labor side; the *Direction de la recherche, des études, de l'évaluation et des statistiques* (Drees) on the health and solidarity side and the *Pôle statistique publique*, a division of the *département des études et statistiques fiscales* (DESF) of the *Direction générale des finances publiques* (DGFiP) on the economy and finance side. All SSM are coordinated by INSEE.

microsimulation. At the turn of the 1990s, despite the experience of the Mir model within the *Direction de la prévision* (Forecasting Branch) some 20 years earlier, static microsimulation was still in its infancy within the *Service de statistique public* (SSP). The data were then a means for the administration to position and assert itself as a specific and legitimate actor in the microsimulation landscape, and in particular in relation to outside researchers. Most of these administrations produce microeconomic data useful for microsimulation, and therefore have direct access to the most up-to-date data. INSEE had access to the latest versions of the ERF for its model named Ines (developed since 1996). Although not part of the SSP, the statistical service of the Cnaf, headed by an INSEE administrator, also had access to the ERF for its Myriade model. For its Saphir model (developed in the early 2000s), the Direction de la Prévision has access to the so-called "heavy" sample of the Direction générale des impôts (equivalent to the "Felin" database, which contains 500,000 tax returns). In a sense, the Forecasting Directorate has an advantage over the INSEE and Cnaf models because of the nature of the data used. It has the capacity to observe income changes from one year to the next and over a more recent period in greater detail. To a certain extent, this asymmetry can be read as a way for these administrations to keep their own resources, which can be mobilized to assert themselves in the expertise of evaluating social and fiscal measures, in the context of social and fiscal measures, both vis-à-vis outside researchers and other administrations (Pénissat 2009). Nevertheless, it should be remembered that INSEE could have used all the tax data in its model, which it has been able to access in theory since 1951, and in fact since 1986[20], and has had access to in order to make up the ERF matching (Legendre et al.

---

20 In its initial version, the 1951 law granted INSEE and the SSM a right of access for statistical production purposes to administrative data of other administrations that were not covered by legal secrecy. The purpose of this right was to lighten the survey work by using information already collected by other administrations. However, the data collected by the tax authorities were protected data (article 2006-2 of the CGI at the time). It was not until the introduction of an article 7 bis to the 1951 law via law no. 86-1305 of December 23, 1986, and article L. 135D of the book of tax procedures that the situation was resolved: "Information relating to natural persons [...] collected [...] by an administration [...] may be transferred, for the sole purpose of compiling statistics, to the National Institute of Statistics and Economic Studies [...] the provisions of the preceding paragraph apply notwithstanding any contrary provisions relating to professional secrecy. professional secrecy. While this is a possibility and not a right ("may be transferred", not "must be ceded"), INSEE can now access the data without the agents of the Ministry of the Economy and Finance being in contradiction with the tax secrecy.

2001). The real gap in data is thus between models internal and external to the administration. Indeed, the most recent data available to researchers are, for the most part, only survey data, whereas the members of the SSP engaged in microsimulation have at least at their disposal at the time of survey data matched with administrative data directly from tax returns, not from survey returns[21]. SSP members also use up-to-date data, where researchers at the time have to make do with less recent data.

	BDF	ERF	POTE	FELIN
	Survey data			
		Administrative data (tax returns)		
Sysiff – Laboratoire Delta	X			
Ines – Insee-Drees-Cnaf		X		
Myriade – Cnaf		X		
Saphir – DG-Trésor		X		
OpenFisca – France Stratégie and Etalab		X		
Taxipp – Institut des politiques publiques		X	X	X

Table 3.1. *Summary of data sources used by each microsimulation model*

Until the early 2000s, researchers thus used informal relationships rather than legal battle to gain access to administrative data. The weakness of the legal framework at the time, which was little known to both researchers and agents, allowed for "greater flexibility in the circulation [of survey data], particularly among researchers" (Pénissat 2009). The latter, however, must most of the time make do with survey data alone, even if obtaining a research contract or agreements with members of the SSP occasionally allow access to survey data matched with administrative data (ERF)[22]. Largely tolerated by the administrations concerned, these practices will eventually backfire on researchers when some of them cross a "red line" from the 2010s

---

21 For example, the Family Budget (*Budget des familles*) survey requires respondents to keep an account book for several days to record all their expenditures (consumption component) and declare their income (income component). Errors or omissions can thus occur in the declarations made by the respondents, directly affecting the quality of the data collected.

22 In other areas, however, some researchers are able to access administrative data by using informal relationships. See, for example, the conditions of access by researchers to Dares databases (Pénissat 2009, pp. 403–404).

onwards: the reuse of data for political purposes in order to participate in public debate. This episode will however open the way to more formalization in data access for researchers, the most advanced form of which to date is the Law for a Digital Republic adopted in 2016.

3.2. The movement to open up at the turn of the 2010s: from retreat to institutional change

The opening of the data of the administration outside of SSM agents follows a particular trajectory. The first "general public" model of the early 2010s used original data compared to previous experiences of microsimulation, but these data were diverted both from their primary purpose and from authorized uses. While this episode rekindled the caution of administrations towards researchers concerning the transmission of sensitive data, several initiatives will subsequently increase the openness from the middle of the 2010s.

3.2.1. *Fiscal revolution and statistical counter-revolution: a movement to close the data*

In the second half of the 1990s, in order to study high incomes in France, Thomas Piketty had access, thanks to a contract with the Direction de la Prévision, to sources that were still difficult for researchers to access at the time: the samples of General Directorate of Taxes (Direction Générale des Impôt (DGI) declarations from 1988 to 1995 and the ERFs from 1970 to 1990 (Piketty 1998). His participation in the Conseil d'analyse économique's report on economic inequalities, published in 2001, gave him a new opportunity to work on these data, while expressing the wish to access exhaustive tax data from the DGI to better account for changes in the situation of the most fortunate. A few years later, while preparing a thesis under his direction, Camille Landais was able to use the exhaustive tax data produced by the tax authorities to update Piketty's series (covering the period 1970–1996) for the period from 1998 to 2005 (Landais 2007). Access to these data allows us to explore the distribution of income at a finer level of detail, which focuses attention on new categories of actors (the richest 1%) and shows a rapid growth in inequality over the period studied by Landais. This result confirms those actors who, surprised by INSEE's previous diagnosis of roughly stable inequalities from one year to the next, argued at the same time for a new approach to inequalities[23].

To this first form of statactivism (affirmation of a collective category), Piketty and Landais soon added a second one (transformation of the conditions of democratic debate), by giving the general public access to a new microsimulation model created for the occasion to allow everyone to simulate their own tax reform[24]. The site accompanies the release of the book *Pour une révolution fiscale* (in which Emmanuel Saez also participates), whose publication a year before the 2012 presidential election (where the label of "president of the rich" already sticks to the outgoing president) does not go unnoticed. To feed their model, the authors once again rely on tax data, in particular the 2006 ERF[25]. The conditions under which all these data were obtained could not be fully clarified. The most likely hypothesis seems to be that of a reutilization of data made available for other projects[26]. Prohibited by the research agreements, which commit the researchers to deleting the files at the end of the project for which they were granted, the practice of reusing data without requesting new authorizations was not exceptional at the time. Above all, this practice could be tolerated all the more as the dissemination of the results produced remained limited to the academic community. Whatever the exact conditions under which the three researchers had access to the ERF for this project, this much more publicized and political use of the data provoked a backlash from the administration.

This situation will complicate access to the databases for researchers who, from 2011 onwards, wished to pursue the development of a new microsimulation model under the name of Taxipp at the Paris School of

---

23 Sujobert (2014) recounts how this criticism, brought to the level of the National Council for Statistical Information, led to the creation of an active working group between mid-2004 and January 2007 and helped INSEE evolve on these issues, making visible the last percentiles below the last decile.

24 See www.revolution-fiscale.fr/simulez-votre-propre-reforme-fiscale.

25 The ERF survey became the *Enquête revenu fiscaux et sociaux* (ERFS) in 2005. For the sake of readability, we will retain the original name "ERF" in the rest of this chapter.

26 In addition to the research projects already mentioned above, we can also mention a thesis defended at the Paris School of Economics in 2009 for which the author had access to the ERF 2006.

Economics[27]. These researchers were increasingly refused requests for hosting conventions (provided for by the 1978 law) to use data produced by administrations directly on their premises. This was all the more problematic because, while the Tax Revolution team had several sources of administrative data (in addition to ERF, the model relied on several survey data: household budgets, assets, housing, employment, etc.)[28], the following teams only had access to the global aggregation of these databases, and not the raw databases, making any further development of the model complex.

3.2.2. From a relationship of distrust to one of trust: the IPP and the LPR/Lemaire law (2011–2016)

This is the blockage faced by the team in charge of developing the Taxipp model, which paradoxically was to be the driving force behind the acceleration of the movement to open up microeconomic data. At the time, the team was headed by Antoine Bozio (director of the *Institut des politiques publiques*, whose initial project was the development of the Taxipp model), and the *Direction générale des finances publiques* (DGFiP) refused to give it access to the ERFS survey data following its request made at the end of 2011[29]. The secrecy imposed by the Book of Tax Procedures was invoked, even though periodic access had been granted previously. With the support of the director of the Comité du secret and the Prime Minister's office at the time, and in particular his economic advisor Fabien Dell, with whom Antoine Bozio had worked in previous research projects (Schulz 2019), a reform process was set in motion to clarify the law concerning access to this data. The Prime Minister's office finally resulted in a bill granting access for research and evaluation purposes. This bill had to be reworked several times: misinterpretation of the law's objectives by the departments in charge of drafting it, retaken by the SGG's legal experts to comply with European law (not creating a monopoly with the Secure Data Access Center, *Centre d'accès sécurisé aux données* – CASD), a project retested as a "budgetary

27 The Taxipp model developed by the *Institut des politiques publiques* (part of the PSE) builds on the programs developed for Tax Revolution (later renamed Taxipp v.0.0).

28 For a detailed presentation of the source files, see the technical appendix available online on the Tax Revolution website.

29 In this section, we rely mainly on an interview conducted with Antoine Bozio in July 2021 and an appendix of his HDR thesis (Bozio 2018, pp. 63–68) in which he presents the steps taken to access the data used for Taxipp.

rider" (cavalier budgétaire[30]) in the 2012 finance bill... It was not until 2013 that the project was finally integrated into the law on higher education and research, and then its implementation in 2014, that the IPP teams were able to access data previously covered by tax secrecy: ERF, as well as the data of the ERF, and also the "heavy" sample of income tax returns. This data was instrumental in the design of Taxipp version 1.0.

Once access to data covered by tax secrecy was authorized, the question of access to Social Security data arose. In 2016, Antoine Bozio explained that he was refused access to data from the national sample of Cnaf beneficiaries, even though he was carrying out an evaluation with his teams for the Cour d'comptes, and that he had been given access to it two years earlier. The breach of professional secrecy is invoked. Despite the support of the director of the social policy division of Matignon, who succeeded in obtaining an agreement from the general management of the Cnaf for the opening of the data, the services had still not transmitted the data several months later. Finally, a new article of law was drafted to "guarantee conditions of legal security for the administrations that would authorize access to their data". The article is inserted in the law for a digital republic known as the "Lemaire law", adopted at the end of 2016. The latter thus provides that administrations are not at fault if they transmit these data to researchers. It thus does not offer a right of access to the researcher: administrations "may", not "must"[31]. However, it turns out that an administration rarely refuses access to data to researchers who would like to carry out studies on the impact of its public policies, since refusal is difficult to assume publicly: "If the law provides that 'administrations may communicate data', this implies that they retain control over the communication of data. But, in practice, a balance is found, and they generally give their consent"[32].

Beyond these developments, the CNIS (Conseil national de l'information statistique/French Statistical Advisory Committee) report co-authored in 2017 by Antoine Bozio and Pierre-Yves Geoffard at the request of the Secretary of State for Digital Affairs in the wake of the LPR law, notes several persistent difficulties in accessing administrative data for research

---

30 *A legislative provision appearing in a Budget Bill but unrelated to it.*
31 The conditions for sharing data between administrations are also facilitated.
32 Interview with Antoine Bozio, July 2021.

purposes. In particular, the LPR provides for access to most data, but not for processing and not always for matching. Only data already used for statistical processing within the administration can be processed by researchers[33]. Data used for management purposes within the administration cannot be processed. The report also notes a widespread misinterpretation of the law by administrations. For example, the CNIL's injunctions[34] not to retain data after use were interpreted as injunctions to destroy the data.

While all is not yet perfect, the initiatives undertaken at the beginning of the 2010s have enabled researchers and administrations to establish relationships of mutual trust, sweeping away the image of "unreliable" researchers, which became prevalent again at the end of the 2000s. The construction of a progressive legal framework until 2016, and in particular the establishment of a Secure Data Access Center (*Centre d'accès sécurisé à distance*, CASD) in 2013, have made it possible to reassure administrations that were afraid to communicate data covered by a secret. This successful institutional transformation contrasts with the more frontal manner in which the codes models were opened, for which "the administration had all the means not to do".

3.3. The movement to open up codes: free consent versus forced freedom

Microeconomic data are essential to run simulations of a model. The code of the model, in particular that of the tax-benefit system, can be reconstructed from the law, but not the micro-economic data. Not having access to the codes of the models should therefore not be blocking for an administration or a team of researchers who would have the databases, and who would like to embark on microsimulation. However, having this code can save precious time, since it allows saving part of the development time of the model (reproducing the legislation in the form of code). A time that required many months, especially to identify and then transcribe the current tax-benefit system. For this reason, several people involved in the development of models both outside and within the administration wished at one time or another to have access to the INSEE model. In particular, when

---

33 For example, court data can be accessed by researchers, but no processing can be done.

34 CNIL: Commission nationale de l'informatique et des libertés/French Data Protection Authority.

the *Institut des politiques publiques* (IPP) was launched, Antoine Bozio wanted to recover the way in which the tax scales were coded, rather than having to redo the entire reconstruction work. Made freely available under the name of "IPP scales", they are part of a general movement to open up codes. The latter are part of a general movement to open up the codes both from within (see section 3.3.1) and from outside the administration (see section 3.3.2.).

3.3.1. *The first steps of an "open source" culture within the administration*

At the end of the 2000s, two economists from the *Centre d'analyse stratégique* placed at the disposal of the Prime Minister (CAS, which has since become France Stratégie) wished to have an instrument for simulating the tax-benefit system. As the CAS is not part of the official statistical service, they do not have access to the most recent versions of the ERF or to the microsimulation models already available within the administration. The two economists decided to develop their own program, called Openfisca[35]. This program initially calculates the amount of taxes and social benefits based on a given individual situation and soon feeds an online simulator for beneficiaries. It will subsequently undergo numerous evolutions, in particular after the association – formal and then informal – of Etalab and the IPP around the model following an order from the Prime Minister's office at the time, followed by Fabien Dell. Sharing the culture of free software, the authors chose from the outset to make their instrument open access, inspired by the regrouping of forces that had occurred in another field:

> Previously in meteorology, all the labs were doing their own model to simulate the world's weather and were exhausted in the race to build the perfect model. One of the labs opened up their model, and everyone started collaborating on the same model. [...] And I said to myself that this is exactly what we're facing today: multiple jurisdictions building their models, competing with each other[36].

---

35 See Shulz (2019) for a detailed discussion of the development of this model.
36 Testimony of one of the two authors of the model cited by Shulz (2019, p. 854).

The code is put online on a contributory platform (Github)[37], which allows us to follow the improvements proposed by a potentially important number of developers, and to check them before integration. The choice to use this platform is also a way for its creators to prevent a later "locking" by the administration[38].

In parallel with the use of an extended community of developers, the two members of the CAS exchanged very early on with the microsimulation teams of INSEE and DREES, who were in favor of sharing the work of updating the tax-benefit system on an annual basis. On the side of these traditional numerical administrations, the renewal of the teams also saw the Ines model pass into the hands of agents more in tune with the philosophy of free software. Schematically, we can distinguish in the different teams in charge of the Ines model since its creation profiles more oriented towards programming, other profiles more oriented towards studies, without this distinction initially overlapping with differences in training. Within the same teams, there are people with comparable backgrounds who are more or less concerned about the approximations made by Ines and more or less willing to produce results or refine the model. The tendency to focus on the model rather than on the production of results was deplored by one of the interviewees with the expression "geek de trop" (i.e. "the over-zealous geek"):

> There was always what I called "the over-zealous geek": it is the person who, wanting to do well, will write pages and pages of program to try to simulate something well, but who will forget that the cost of entry for others will increase and that finally there is also a risk of error (Interview with a member of the INES-Insee team).

What appears to the "data geek" to be an essential, even common sense, improvement can be perceived as an additional source of complexity for other team members. This discrepancy can be seen in the way in which a new redesign of the program in the early 2010s was assessed, at the sole initiative of the INSEE team, which not only had to convince its hierarchy

---

37 See Chapter 4 for a perspective on digital innovation platforms.
38 Interview with the second author of the model, August 2020.

but also had to overcome the reservations of the DREES team[39]. This change took place at a time when the INSEE and DREES teams were content to transmit their program modifications by e-mail, which could create discrepancies between the versions handled by each side. These coordination failures were overcome by an organizational change made possible by a technological catch-up. Starting in 2014, the INSEE and DREES teams used the online platform Adullact[40] to share the model by keeping track of the successful versions of the programs, so as to be able to both directly integrate all the modifications of pieces of program into a single version of Ines and easily go back at any time. Again, this was a common sense idea from a software developer's point of view, since the use of versioning software was already common practice outside the administration at that time. The initiative came from an INSEE administrator with an atypical profile, since she joined Ensae while preparing a doctorate in theoretical and mathematical physics, at a time when the "data science" courses at Ensae had not yet been created. During her time in the Social Studies Division, she worked on optimizing Ines, so that what used to run for two hours ended up running for less than a quarter of an hour[41], allowing for new generations of studies[42]. Her experience convinced the management of INSEE of the usefulness of temporarily creating an additional post for an IT profile to continue developing the model.

Between the beginning of the 2000s and the middle of the following decade, the figure of the "the over-zealous geek" gave way to the more highly valued figure of the "data scientist" who managed to demonstrate the interest of continuing to invest in code while at the same time making coordination between teams more fluid, thereby making it possible to forge

---

39 This new version of Ines is less easy to access because it breaks with the linear logic that prevailed until now by multiplying the program bits called at different places in a master file. This structure appears obvious to the following "geeks", who would tend to relativize the extent of the change, and not very intuitive to others. An evolution that has enriched the potential of the tool, notably by allowing the application of the tax-benefit rule of different years to the same database. But it also required a significant amount of time to appropriate and control the consequences of all the changes.

40 Association of developers and users of free software for administrations and local authorities.

41 Two hours to run the entire program, including updating the database. This result is also partly due to the implementation of central servers at INSEE.

42 In particular, the calculation of the advanced poverty indicator, which immediately became an established part of the public statistics landscape.

new ties with new microsimulation teams, motivated on the one hand by a broader conception of official statistics, and on the other hand by the philosophy of free software. Facilitated by the move to Adullact, the opening of Ines is defended by the agents in charge of the model on the basis of arguments of various kinds:

> It was really a desire on the part of both INSEE and DREES agents to participate in this movement towards open source, to increase global knowledge, with the idea that it could also be useful to us, because users could participate in updating or improving the code. To be very honest on this point, we have not seen huge gains for us, except for one very important gain, a gain in reputation: the OFCE, for example, gave us a lot of publicity by saying that this opening was a major innovation for statistics in the 21st century. And then behind that too, there is the fact that it is too expensive to have so many microsimulation models, and so we thought that there was probably going to be a time when there would be a gathering, and so it was better to make Ines available as quickly as possible to make it more widely known (Interview with Michael Sicsic, responsible for the Ines model at Insee from 2015 to 2020, July 2020).

The beginning of the reflections on the opening of Ines dates back to 2012, even before the move to Adullact. The model was opened in 2016[43]. In the meantime, the exchanges with the OpenFisca developers were abruptly interrupted by other free software activists with a more offensive mode of action. They will push for a generalized opening of microsimulation models.

3.3.2. *Forced openness: the administration ordered to communicate or open up the codes of its microsimulation models*

In 2014, a young economist was doing his internship at the *Secrétariat général de modernisation de l'action publique* (SGMAP), and more specifically in the Etalab department[44] in charge of coordinating and

---

43 https://adullact.net/projects/ines-libre/.
44 See Goëta (2017) for an overview of this structure created in 2011.

implementing the State's strategy for opening up administrative data, contributing to the development of OpenFisca (a partnership was concluded at the time between its designers within the CAS and Etalab). His task was to transcript into code the legislation concerning the tax and benefit system. Rather than recoding this legislation entirely, he envisaged directly using the calculator used to collect the tax[45]. His initial direct requests denied, he began engaging in judiciary proceedings in May 2015. He did not use a lawyer and went to court without any particular means at his disposal. He took his case to the Cada, then to the administrative court, and finally obtained the code in question in May 2017, one week before the final deliberation, i.e. 20 months after beginning his approach.

Meanwhile, the General Directorate of Public Finance organized a hackathon in April 2016 (Algan et al. 2016). Bringing together nearly 150 participants from both the administration and civil society (companies, researchers and "ordinary" citizens), and organized with Etalab, the purpose of these two days was to imagine possible uses outside the administration for the source code of the tax calculator. The current legal proceedings were not mentioned by the Minister of Finance and Public Accounts at the time, Michel Sapin, nor by the Secretary of State for the Budget, Christian Eckert, nor by the Secretary of State for Digital Affairs, Axelle Lemaire (who was in charge of the law for a Digital Republic, presented to the Council of Ministers a few days earlier). Instead, the latter emphasizes the fact that "the opening of a source code of a computer by an administration is a first [...] this step [...] is the image of an open and responsible State, which considers that the management of our 'common good' is not a prerogative of the administration, but that it is a responsibility of all"[46].

In any case, the approach taken with the Cada made jurisprudence[47], and directly inspired the creation of an association a few months later: the Ouvre-boîte. Created on March 6, 2017, the purpose of this association is to obtain "access to the effective publication of administrative documents, and

---

45 The latter tells, in the form of a tutorial, why and how he undertook to request the opening of this code on the forum of Etalab: https://forum.etalab.gouv.fr/t/howto-obtenir-dune-administration-lacces-a-un-code-source/186.

46 Discours d'introduction d'Axelle Lemaire, April 1, 2016 [Online]. Available: https://www.economie.gouv.fr/files/files/PDF/discours_axellelemaire_hackathon.pdf.

47 Microsimulation models are now considered administrative documents and can be made available to anyone who requests them.

more particularly of data, databases and source codes, in accordance with the sources, in accordance with the texts in force"[48]. Its members coordinate their activity via different web platforms (information wiki, discussion forum), and have defined rules in order to optimize their coordination and limit the risks of errors[49]:

> He went through the whole process without any outside help, he wrote his application, his brief... L'Ouvre-boîte didn't exist, and he proved that it was possible to activate the legal levers without having big means. We took up the same method, which we continued over time [...]. This example proved to us that the steps necessary to open documents require limited energy (Excerpt from an interview with a member of the Ouvre-boîte, July 2019).

The source codes are now considered as administrative documents like any other. The association undertakes requests to obtain (successfully) the opening of the tax calculators, and even obtained the complete opening of three years of IR and ISF[50] calculators. Even before the Cada request, Etalab, which was created by decree in 2011, was already known for pushing administrations to open their data using the Open Data argument. Requests in this sense had already been made directly to the microsimulation teams as well as to their hierarchy.

But like the Tax Revolution simulator, the request to open the tax code via the Cada will make administrations nervous. As this request comes from a person in charge of contributing to the development of Openfisca, discussions between the microsimulation teams at Insee-Drees and Openfisca have broken down. Moreover, the latter are critical of the "knife to the throat" method, thinking that the method was approved by the Etalab department. Etalab explains that the process was initiated by the person in question, and that the internal policy of the director at the time was to maintain good relations with other administrations, particularly with Bercy:

---

48 Announcement no. 1903, p. 113, published in the *Journal officiel* establishing the association.

49 https://ouvre-boite.org.

50 Income tax (IR) and wealth tax (ISF).

And then there was the history of Cada requests, which deteriorated all the dialogue there was [...]. The first request for access was for the tax source code, I think [...]. Well, I think that was the last time we had Etalab in the working groups. I think it made everyone tense that we were discussing on one side and on the other side, they put the knife under the throat [...]: "You don't want to work with us, well, we'll force you in fact" (Interview with Ines team member, July 2020).

The association Ouvre-boîte was founded a few months after this Cada request by, among others, the supervisor of the person who initiated it. After that, the association undertakes several dozens of code opening projects on a multitude of subjects. Among them, requests for the opening of one of INSEE's dynamic microsimulation models, Destinie, only a few months before the release in Open Access on the Adullact platform of the INSEE-Drees static microsimulation model.

The requests to open models are motivated by a primary reason, which is, for the members of the association, a form of democratic statactivism democratic: to be able to freely audit the administration and reuse the models it develops with public money, to contribute to the public debate (political parties, journalism, decoders, economists' offices, research laboratories, etc.).

The mode of intervention based on direct confrontation with the administration is clearly assumed, for the sake of efficiency: according to its members, the administration does not always lend itself to the game, it is not worth consuming time to, for example, assist it in a possible openness method:

With our very limited means, we only do what is strictly necessary. This makes us grumpy in the eyes of the administrations. Moreover, it is difficult to build a relationship of trust and at the same time to bring a lawsuit. Other civil society actors try to establish a dialogue, but find themselves limited in their means of action. The legal orientation of the association frees us from such remorse, but often shackles us in a confrontational relationship (Interview with a member of the Ouvre-boîte, July 2019).

Document designation	Holding Authority	Request date	Opening date
Bilan GES	ADEME	02/03/2020	11/06/2021
Inventaire du patrimoine naturel	OFB-CNRS	05/01/2021	05/01/2021
Comptes	Sciences Po	18/11/2018	18/03/2021
Données de trafic SURF3	Ville de Paris	28/12/2018	25/07/2020
Base carbone	ADEME	02/03/2020	28/05/2020
Données du budget	Direction du budget	09/05/2018	12/05/2019
Bases de l'Inpi	Inpi	29/05/20 217	17/04/2019
Modèle Mélèze	Insee	15/11/2017	26/03/2019
Cartes géologiques " Bd Charm-50"	Brgm	08/04/2018	07/03/2019
Modèle Omphale2010	Insee	15/11/2017	21/12/2018
Modèle Myriade*	Cnaf	15/11/2017	27/09/2019
Modèle Destinie2	Insee	08/11/2017	20/09/2018
Modèle Saphir	DG Trésor	08/11/2017	05/09/2018
Modèle Mésange	DG Trésor	08/11/2017	05/09/2018
Catalogue des collections des musées de France Joconde (extrait)	Musées de France	14/05/2017	03/04/2018
Cadastre	DGFiP	27/06/2017	29/09/2017
Calculette de l'impôt sur le revenu	DGFiP	04/05/2017	14/09/2017

* The Myriade model has not been appealed to the Cada (a first appeal has been addressed to the Ministry of Health, which does not have control over the model).

Table 3.2. *Successful applications made by the Ouvre-boîte association since its creation and that have been successful, classified by decreasing date of acceptance (source: website of the association)*

This positioning allows certain actors who would not want to lose good relations with the administration a framework for forcing the opening without having to expose themselves publicly – the steps can be taken and signed by another member of the association. The members of the association are rather discreet, apart from a few former members of Etalab who are among the original members of the association. This can be explained by the personal convictions of these agents, and not by Etalab's desire to have an organization that would allow it to formulate Cada requests (as a reminder, Etalab itself could not formulate requests to the Cada, as the latter does not rule on interadministration relations; appeals must also be made by a natural person). Moreover, the association considers that these requests constitute a form of acculturation to the administrations. By relying on the LPR law of 2016, which allows many data and codes to be opened by default, the bet is taken that the requests made to the administrations will make them aware that "it is not so complicated to apply the Open Data by default" (excerpt from an interview with a representative of the Ouvre-boîte, July 2019).

What consequences have these requests had on the way the models are opened, within the General Directorate of the Treasury (Saphir model) and the Cnaf (Myriade model)? At Cnaf, the model was abandoned several months ago, so opening up the model was not an issue for the administration. The only reticence came from the feeling of "wasting time". On the DG Trésor (French treasury) side, some of the agents were in favor of this opening to offer more accountability and transparency to citizens. Another party was reluctant, anticipating the "problems" that management would face if the software were opened up (which were already present during the discussions on opening up the Insee-Drees model): counter-simulations to be produced in order to disprove a misuse of the software, verification of all the French treasury's previous work (and therefore detection of potential errors, which would taint the administration's credibility), attacks from the press, etc. In the end, the solution initially adopted by the French treasury, both for its Saphir microsimulation model and for the other models for which requests were made (Mésange and Opale) by the Ouvre-boîte, was to stick to strict compliance with the law, without taking advantage of the opportunity to adopt a more voluntary approach comparable to that of INSEE. However, more recently, the French treasury seems to have evolved on this issue. Since June 2021, he has made available on his website an actualized programs of the Opale macroeconomic model and has been more willing to communicate, via social networks, about the availability of their model, which could bring them some benefits in terms of image[51].

---

51 Tresthor : le nouvel outil de la DG Trésor pour réaliser des prévisions macroéconomiques [Online]. Available at: https://www.tresor.economie.gouv.fr/Articles/2021/06/30/tresthor-the-dg-treasury's-new-tool-for-macroeconomic-forecasting. The tone of this article published by the DG Trésor on June 30, 2021, accompanied by a communication on social networks carried out by its chief economist, among others, contrasts with the communication carried out three years earlier for the openings forced by the Ouvre-boîte: https://www.tresor.economie.gouv.fr/Articles/2018/09/05/la-dg-tresor-met-a-la-disposition-du-public-les-codes-sources-des-modeles-mesange-opale-et-saphir.

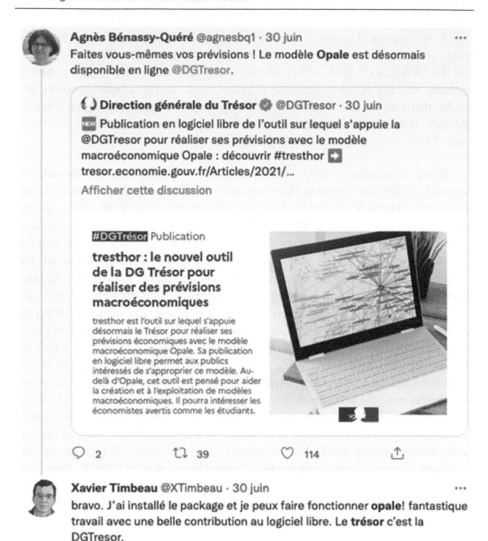

Figure 3.2. *The Director of the DG Trésor tweets about the release of a complement to one of her models. A researcher of the OFCE reacts (June 2021)[52]. For a color version of this figure, see www.iste.co.uk/revest/digital.zip*

---

52 Source: Twitter.fr.

COMMENT ON FIGURE 3.2.– Agnès Bénassy-Quéré @agnesbq1 – 30 June "Do your own forecasts! The OPALE model is now available online @DGTresor". Directorate General of the Treasury (France) @DGTresor – 30 June "Publication as free software, the tool which the French Treasury uses to produce its forecasts with the macroeconomic model Opale: discover now #tresthor > tresor.economie.gouv.fr/Articles/2021/..." View this thread: #DGTrésor Publication "tresthor: the new tool which the French Treasury uses to produce macroeconomic forecasts tresthor is the tool which the Treasury uses to produce economic forecasts using the macroeconomic model Opale. Its release as a free software allows interested parties to use this model for themselves. Beyond Opale, this tool was developed to support the creation and exploitation of macroeconomic models. It could be of interest to informed economists such as students." Xavier Timbeau @XTimbeau - 30 June "bravo. I have installed the package and now I can operate Opale! Fantastic work and a great contribution to free software. The Treasury are the real treasure here!".

This proactive policy of the French treasury can be seen as a sign that the strategy of forcing openness in order to change the culture of the administrations would be successful. After a first series of "forced" openings, the DG Trésor has committed by itself to putting these updated programs online. On the other hand, this could also be seen as following the path shown by the Ines team in opening its model spontaneously; or as the fact that the challenge is now shifting from opening to the valorization of Open Data. If it is not possible to decide on one or the other of these readings, we would now like to enrich this reflection with a more global look at the results obtained by the various ways of obtaining codes and data.

3.4. Discussion: different conceptions of opening up quality?

Finally, we would like to debate the different demands for openness made by the protagonists of this story and to understand, from the results obtained so far, the interest of the different approaches undertaken for potential users of microsimulation models. More generally, the study of these two dimensions allows us to understand the coexistence of several conceptions of quality of openness. In other words, there are different ways of defining what openness is.

This survey first allowed us to reveal the tension between two expectations regarding the availability of codes of microsimulation models from the administration: transparency and accessibility. On the accessibility hand, "opening up well" consists of making the code usable. This conception, which seems to be the most common, is put forward by the authors of one of the very first guides to Open Data published in France (Chignard and Marchandise 2012). It also motivated an investment of the members of the Ines team when they opened their model[53]. In addition to writing a presentation leaflet for their microsimulation tool, these proponents of the open-source model had to modify their programmes to meet this accessibility requirement. First, they added additional comments to make the code clearer for users outside administrations. Second, they stopped using variables in the ERF not available outside the official statistical service (including the Quetelet Network). This includes for example "indirectly nominative" information that might in some cases allow a particular individual to be identified by cross-checking. One the hand of transparency, some microsimulation teams (Myriade and Saphir), contracted to open up their model to external requests, have instead been content to make the existing code available without worrying about the possibilities of using it and about the possibilities of further use[54]. This second way of opening up is more in line with the expectations of the association l'Ouvre-boîte, which focuses on the strict application of the law. Guided by a requirement for transparency, its members consider that opening up well is above all about delivering the raw code, as used in the law, without restriction. Under these conditions, the administration is not expected to provide an explanatory note or to "clean up" its code. This can be interpreted as a way to hide imperfections and information. In fact, one of the fears raised by the project to open was that the teams would be overwhelmed with requests for public justification. The main effort made by Cnaf at the time of the constrained

---

53 The accessibility requirement would even require that teams abandon the proprietary software on which their model is based (SAS) to ensure true openness. This is indeed what they are doing (by switching to R) but for other considerations (budgétaires), independent of the openness project.

54 Unlike Ines (Albouy et al. 2003 and the regular boxes in publications produced from the model) and Myriade (Legendre et al. 2001; Marc and Pucci 2011), Saphir had not, until its opening, Saphir had not been the subject of any publication presenting it. As a result, the DG Trésor nevertheless wrote a note presenting the model when it was opened (Amoureux et al. 2018), again with less attention than for Ines.

opening up of Myriade was to check that the entire program does not have elements in the comments that could be challenged.

Beyond the absence of retouching of transmitted documents, the conception of what should be a good opening up guided by the requirement of transparency presupposes the absence of any barrier to their consultation. In this respect, the conditions of access to the Ines model have also been criticized. To access the program, external users must create an account on the Adullact platform and then request to join the "Ines libre" project, which limits the openness of the model for some members of the Ouvre-boîte association:

> It can be accessed after a period of time, which is indefinite since there is a manual validation. If the validating person is on vacation, it may take some time. This is not in accordance with the texts, and it irritates those who are accustomed to the uses of open source communities. Another problem, if the access is not anonymous: it is a restriction which is not provided for by the texts either and which goes against open source practices (Extract from an interview with a representative of Ouvre-boîte, July 2019).

From the point of view of the INSEE and DREES microsimulation teams, one of the objectives of opening up Ines was to create a community of users who could make improvements to the model. The existence of this community can be facilitated by knowing the people who access the model, and most of them are well identified by an INSEE team leader whom we interviewed. However, the registration procedure allows users to remain anonymous.

If we now look at the effects produced by the different opening requests, we can distinguish two strategies (forcing the opening/gaining the trust of the administration) and two priority targets (codes/donations). In terms of microsimulation, the Ouvre Boîte's strategy focused on codes and sought to force the opening of which it sought to force open. The most significant result was probably the publication online of the microsimulation model still used today by the DG Trésor. Apart from the agents of this directorate, few people knew what the architecture of the model looked like and how a particular device was precisely quantified by the French treasury. This non-transparency which could be explained by the fact that, unlike INSEE or

DREES, the DG Trésor carries out most of its work in response to orders from the minister's office[55].

From now on, anyone can download the 15 programs that make up the model with a single click on the DG Trésor's website and consult, for example, the way in which non-take-up of the activity allowance and the RSA is simulated (program 14), directly in SAS (the priority software under which runs the model) as well as from any text file reader. The interest of being able to read the program in this way appears limited, however, in the eyes of the microsimulation actors outside the administration that we were able to interview, whether it be a member of the IPP who develops their own model or even a member of the OFCE who was nevertheless pleased, at the time of the opening of Ines, to be able to retrieve the data from the Ines model, to be able to recover a model from the administration[56]:

> Unlike Saphir, Ines is not forced open, it is made available, which makes a big difference. In November, when the Ines team provides the legislation for the year N-1, it runs: you have the right ERF dataframe, you hit "Enter", and the model [...] calculates all the aggregates. Whereas for Saphir, you just have code. [Now] to evaluate a code you have to be able to execute it, and [therefore], what is essential is to have as input the data in the format used by the code.

Other reasons are also put forward by Antoine Bozio to relativize the importance of codes, while hardening the divide between interest in the code and interest in data.

> I don't see the opening of the Saphir code obtained by the Ouvre-boîte as something essential [...]. For me, the main information is not the code, but the underlying data [...]. In microsimulation, there are those who believe in the code and those who believe in the data. Those who believe in the code think that it is by making test-cases that we understand what

---

55 However, the Treasury's General Directorate does carry out research and studies, in particular for the academic journal *Économie & Prévision*, which it publishes. It has also intensified its external communication more recently through its thematic notes.

56 Pierre Madec and Xavier Timbeau, Statistique publique: une révolution silencieuse, OFCE le blog, 2017.

happens [...]. But that's misleading because you don't know where the mass of households or individuals are in the distribution. So you can look at test-cases that don't exist! [...] What we absolutely need to know are the characteristics of households in order to understand how many are affected by this or that measure. And for that, we need detailed data on all households [...]. If we compare Ines and Taxipp on the basis of their code, we will not find any substantial differences, whereas on the basis of the underlying data, the information available may be really different (Interview with Antoine Bozio, July 2021).

As we have seen, this vision is not only that of a microsimulator outside the administration but also a vision of the main entrepreneurs of the thawing of relations between researchers and members of the SSP, for access to the latter's data by the former. Their action reflects a different form of statactivism, as different from that of their predecessors, who favored circumventing certain rules (not reusing data obtained for a specific project for other projects), as from that of the datactivists, who favor confrontation by relying on other rules (going to the Cada and then to the administrative court to opening up the data). This other strategy is based on a cross between the "bargain and discussion" strategy described by sociological neo-institutionalists, and the "implementation-appropriation" (Pressman and Wildasky 1973) of its values through a series of proximity interactions. It is thus based on the idea that, "for this to work, we must not fight again the administrations, but gain their trust" because "the administration has all the means not to do". Note that this posture cannot be reduced simply to a question of temperament. On the contrary, it requires relational resources (proximity to members of cabinets who themselves have the legitimacy to act on these issues, in this case via the legislative instrument) and specific institutional resources (Antoine Bozio is an academic at the head of a research institute of a Parisian grande école, which has the specific ambition of being one of the main players in microsimulation). These resources are not the same as those available to the members of the association l'Ouvre-boîte, even if some of them are members of the administration. The repertoire of action that can be mobilized thus appears more naturally to be the use of the legal framework and its coercive dimension; all the more so as going through an associative structure allows them not to act in their own name, and thus to preserve their position within the administration.

In the less cooperative logic that prevails for the other two strategies, the parties bypassed – or attacked "with the Ouvre-boîte" – can also mobilize other legal resources to defend themselves and thwart the opening. The French treasury was thus able to hide behind the argument of the secrecy of the government's deliberations to deliver only part of its programs (the basic model) and to keep the codes developed in Saphir to simulate different reform projects. Asked in turn by the Ouvre-boîte association to publish their codes, the members of the OFCE have successfully mentioned the intellectual property rights of researchers to keep their models closed. This parry avoids that the association's steps raise new legal questions regarding access to the results of public–private research partnerships. This unexpected turn of events has made researchers, who seemed to be the ones who could benefit most from the struggles of opening-up activists, both the new targets and one of the main barriers to the generalization of this movement.

Finally, and in a more general perspective, the history of the opening of microsimulation models and their data makes it possible to pose in other terms the question of the rationalization of resources – and of the efforts mobilized to assess public action in the light of digital tools, as well as of the boundaries of the State's expertise in evaluation. On the one hand, administrations seem to be progressively moving towards a consolidation around a single model. The regular updating of the model born these indeed requires the mobilization of several agents, and the maintenance of different models within the administrations – which may have been of some interest for identifying the first errors at the beginning of their use, but seems less and less justified. And this is all the more true in a context of budgetary constraints and a continuous search for optimization of existing resources, which was already prevalent at the time of the first opening movements (Pénissat 2009). On the other hand, Open Data offers actors outside of the "historical" data administrations the possibility of providing evaluative expertise of comparable robustness to that produced by the latter, provided they have access to the necessary resources. If they do not produce their own model, these players can even participate directly in the contact with the administration of the model via *open source* version management platforms. In fact, the question of rationalization arises both within administrations and outside of them, since they now have not one but several models developed and updated.

In the end, does not knowing how to open well also mean knowing how to close? If the answer to this question seems to be largely affirmative for most of the people interviewed, the question arises as to which models to close. From the point of view of the user of the opening-up and collaborative administration model (Ines), the latter can be seen as the model "to be kept" for reasons of historic and legitimacy in the certification of the conforming code. From the point of view of the user of an open source model developed outside the public statistics service (Openfisca, used by the latest version of Taxipp), the arguments relate rather to the technical quality of the simulations (quality of the code and data quality), in addition to simplified reuse and a larger user community.

Without taking sides on either position (each of the communities anticipating in the medium term the abandonment of the others models), we note that the French National Assembly recently chose to put the LexImpact microsimulator[57], developed from Open fisca, in the hands of parliamentarians. A sign that this instrument is now more than an "institutional experiment conducted by political hackers at the margins of administration" (Schulz 2019). A middle way is thus emerging: the use of a common base developed by all (tax-benefit system); with a differentiated implementation according to the accessible data and the desired uses, whether it is to quantify an amendment, test a reform or evaluate the action of the government.

3.5. References

Albouy, V., Bouton, F., Le Minez, S., Pucci, M. (2003). Le modèle de microsimulation Ines : un outil d'analyse des politiques socio-fiscales. *Dossiers solidarité et santé*, 3, 23–43.

Algan, Y., Bacache-Beauvallet, M., Perrot, A. (2016). Administration numérique. *Notes du conseil d'analyse économique*, 34(7), 1–12.

Amoureux, V., Benoteau, I., Naouas, A. (2018). Le modèle de microsimulation Saphir. Working document, DG Trésor.

---

57 As of January 2022, the model, which is still under development, makes it possible to microsimulate a reform of income tax, allocations to municipalities, social contributions and benefits, and the CSG. It differs from other models in that it proposes to carry out evaluations from an interface that allows the user to directly modify the articles of the laws concerned.

Béranger, J. (2017). Quelle éthique pour une approche ouverte et communautaire de l'utilisation des big data en santé ? [Online]. Available at: https://medium.com/epidemium/quelle-%C3%A9thique-pour-une-approche-ouverte-et-communau taire-de-lutilisation-des-big-data-en-sant%C3%A9-e9c026881961   [Accessed   27 October 2021].

Bessis, F. and Cotton, P. (2021). La réforme, le chiffrage, son modèle et ses données. Les évolutions du monopole de l'expertise économique au prisme d'un instrument de microsimulation de la législation sociofiscale. *Politix*, 134(2), 7–32.

Blanchet, D., Hagneré, C., Legendre, F., Thibault, F. (2015). Microsimulations statique et dynamique appliquées aux politiques fiscales et sociales : modèles et méthodes. *Économie et statistique*, 481(1), 5–30.

Bozio, A. (2018). Économie publique de la protection sociale. HDR Thesis, Aix-Marseille Université, Marseille.

Bozio, A. and Geoffard, P.-Y. (2017). L'accès des chercheurs aux données administratives. Report, Conseil national de l'information statistique, Paris.

Bruno, I., Didier, E., Prévieux, J. (2014). *Statactivisme : comment lutter avec des nombres*. La Découverte, Paris.

Caporali, A., Morisset, A., Legleye, S., Richou, C. (2015). La mise à disposition des enquêtes quantitatives en sciences sociales : l'exemple de l'Ined. *Population*, 70(3), 567–597.

Chenu, A. (2011). Introduction. In *La France dans les comparaisons internationales. Guide d'accès aux grandes enquêtes statistiques en sciences sociales*, Chenu, A. and Lesnard, L. (eds). Presses de Sciences Po, Paris.

Chignard, S. and Marchandise, J.-F. (2012). *L'Open data : comprendre l'ouverture des données publiques*. FYP éditions, Paris.

Cobb, R.W. and Elder, C.D. (1972). *Participation in American Politics. The Dynamics of Agenda-Building*. Johns Hopkins University Press, Baltimore.

Concialdi, P. (2014). Le BIP40 : alerte sur la pauvreté ! In *Statactivisme : comment lutter avec des nombres*, Bruno, I., Didier, E., Prévieux, J. (eds). La Découverte, Paris.

Goëta, S. (2015). Un air de famille : les trajectoires parallèles de l'open data et du big data. *Informations sociales*, 191(5), 26–34.

Goëta, S. (2017). Une petite histoire d'Etalab : comment l'open data s'est institutionnalisé en France ? *Statistique et société*, 5(3), 11–17.

Landais, C. (2007). Les hauts revenus en France (1998–2006) : une explosion des inégalités ? Working document, Paris School of Economics.

Landais, C., Piketty, T., Saez, E. (2011). *Pour une révolution fiscale : un impôt sur le revenu pour le XXIe siècle*. Le Seuil, Paris.

Legendre, F. (2019). L'émergence et la consolidation des méthodes de microsimulation en France. *Économie et statistique*, 510–512, 201–217.

Legendre, F., Lorgnet, J.-P., Thibault, F. (2001). Myriade : le modèle de microsimulation de la CNAF. Un outil d'évaluation des politiques sociales. *Revue des politiques sociales et familiales*, 66(1), 33–50.

Marc, C. and Pucci, M. (2011). Une nouvelle version du modèle de microsimulation Myriade : trimestrialisation des ressources et évaluation du revenu de Solidarité active. *Dossiers d'études de la Cnaf*, 137.

Pénissat, E. (2009). L'État des chiffres : sociologie du service de statistique et des statisticiens du ministère du Travail et de l'Emploi (1945–2008). Sociology PhD Thesis, EHESS, Paris.

Piketty, T. (1999). Les hauts revenus face aux modifications des taux marginaux supérieurs de l'impôt sur le revenu en France, 1970–1996. *Économie & prévision*, 138(2), 25–60.

Pressman, J.L. and Wildavsky, A.B. (1973). *Implementation*. University of California Press, Berkeley.

Rhein, C. (2002). Démogéographie et données statistiques. *Espace populations sociétés*, 20(1), 125–132.

Shulz, S. (2019). Un logiciel libre pour lutter contre l'opacité du système sociofiscal. *Revue française de science politique*, 69(5), 845–868.

Silberman, R. (2011). *La protection des données individuelles en France et la recherche en sciences sociales*. Presses de Sciences Po, Paris.

Sujobert, B. (2014). Comment intervenir sur le programme de la statistique publique ? L'exemple des inégalités sociales. In *Statactivisme : comment lutter avec des nombres*, Bruno, I., Didier E., Prévieux J. (eds). La Découverte, Paris.

Landais, C. (2007). Les hauts revenus en France (1998-2006) : une explosion des inégalités ?, Working document, Paris School of Economics.

Landais, C., Piketty, T., Saez, J. (2011). Pour une révolution fiscale, un impôt sur le revenu pour le XXI siècle, Le Seuil, Paris.

Lagneau, ... (2019). L'émergence et la consolidation des politiques de ... inflation en France, Economie et Statistique, 26...

How to Characterize Public Innovation Platforms? Crossed Perspectives

In recent years, new information and communication technologies have become a strategic resource for public organizations, to the point of considering the emergence of an "e-government platform" (Chevallier 2018). To enable more efficient management and to meet the need for innovation, public actors are increasingly adopting open innovation models through digital platforms. These platforms can be defined as virtual places of exchange – commercial or not – based on Web 2.0. While they have been massively developed by private companies until now, mobilized technologies offer public organizations the opportunity to amplify creativity and collaboration, and have a strong potential to transform public action. For example, recent works in political science by Hautamäki and Oksanen (2018), Mergel et al. (2019) or Mergel (2020) illustrate the capacity of digital transformation to impact the delivery, and sometimes the efficiency of public services. The new digital tools can also promote greater transparency[1], interoperability and citizen satisfaction (in terms of ease of access or quality of services rendered), and also a reinforced circulation and sharing of public data.

In this chapter, we propose, from an interdisciplinary approach, to address the potentialities offered to public decision-makers by digital platforms in order to conduct various policies, whether they relate to health,

Chapter written by Isabelle LIOTARD, Valérie REVEST and Claudine GAY.

1 See Robert's (2019) critiques of the mobilization of the notion of transparency by the European Commission.

the sharing of Open Data or more specifically on innovation (Chevallier 2018). If from the viewpoint of economic sciences, platforms are essentially understood as specific markets at the heart of complex network effects, from the point of view of management sciences, the notion of platform characterizes the emergence of new organizational forms, constitutes the basis of new business models and becomes a place of excellence for open innovation (OI). However, the conditions of emergence, functioning and transformation (or even disappearance) of platforms forms are not (or hardly) studied by these disciplinary approaches. Engineering sciences and information systems sciences[2] can, at least in part, fill this gap by approaching the platform through design and development methods. From this perspective, the design, operation and continuous improvement of platforms are at the center of the concerns. In fact, studying these aspects can lead to the linking of technical and functional aspects, on the one hand, and the design and implementation of public actions and policies, on the other hand. This leads us to mention the potentialities offered by platforms which are not always well understood by public decision-makers wishing to mobilize or develop them. The objective of this chapter is twofold. On the one hand, we wish to highlight the interest of considering digital innovation platforms from several perspectives: economic, managerial and via the prism of engineering sciences. On the other hand, we want to make public decision-makers aware of the challenges of designing and using this type of tool in the conduct of public policies.

The first section presents the characteristics and challenges of digital platforms, based on work in economics and management sciences. It highlights two main forms (transaction platforms and innovation platforms), which are often combined within platform-companies, creating multiple ecosystems. Beyond these two most widespread forms, the second section explores the functioning of another type of platform that positions itself as an intermediary: the innovation intermediation platform, which has the specificity of being governed by private companies or public bodies. Based on the comparison of two innovation intermediation platforms, one developed by a private company (Innocentive) and the other by a public authority (Challenge.Gov), this section contributes to highlighting the particularities of public platforms and their potential. The third section

---

2 The Information System (IS) is considered here as a field of study of engineering sciences. Hereafter, we will refer only to the engineering sciences.

highlights the contribution of engineering sciences, in particular the lifecycle model, in order to account for the different stages of the implementation of a platform. The final section concludes with a discussion on the perspective of such a multidisciplinary approach.

4.1. Platforms in economics and management

4.1.1. *From the platform to the digital platform: definitions and characteristics*

The term "platform" comes essentially from the world of business and its organization. It was initially used in the context of production platforms (de Reuver et al. 2018), which exist in different forms: (1) internal platforms that allow for the recombination of sub-units within the company, (2) supply chain platforms coordinating external suppliers around an assembler, and (3) industry platforms where the platform leader pools the external capabilities of complementors (Gawer 2014). While the platform initially characterized the internal organization of the firm, over time it has been extended to devices open to the outside of the firm, benefiting from the contributions of digital technology.

For example, if a company creates and offers a "hub" that other companies can in turn mobilize, the main purpose of the platform is to connect different categories of actors. As an example, Atos announced on July 7, 2021 the launch of *Atos Digital Hub*, a solution whose main purpose is to serve as an accelerator for the design of platforms ecosystems[3].

Among the possible forms, digital platforms occupy an important place in our economies. They emerged with the advent of the Internet in the 2000s and remain the focus of many academic studies to this day (Evans and Gawer 2016; Teece 2017; Hein et al. 2020). Gafa (Google, Amazon, Apple, Facebook), travel and accommodation booking sites (Booking, Airbnb), ride-hailing platforms (Blablacar, Uber) and online commerce more generally (Vinted, Leboncoin, etc.) are part of a new ecosystem (Lusch and Nambisan 2015), leading some authors to call them "platform-companies" (Gawer 2021).

---

3 https://www.usine-digitale.fr/article/atos-lance-l-atos-digital-hub-une-solution-pour-faciliter-le-partage-de-donnees.N1122784.

Digital platforms, mainly developed by the private sector, have been the subject of an abundant literature whose objective is to try to identify their contours and main characteristics. A recent definition has been proposed by Teece (2017). Digital platforms are considered as entities that "provide common standards, interfaces, and tools to amplify the impact of key technologies to increase the productivity and profitability of a company, a group of companies, or users" (Teece 2017, p. 2). According to this approach, digital platforms can be understood based on three common characteristics: they are technology-driven, they facilitate interactions between different groups of users (whether they are in a position of supply or demand) and they support the execution of defined tasks (Gawer 2009; Cusumano et al. 2019; Koskinen et al. 2019). Moreover, the specificity of digital platforms (compared to traditional non-digital platforms) (2018): they constitute a set of digital resources (including services and content), encouraging the interactions that create value between external producers and consumers (Constantinides et al. 2018).

Cusumano et al. (2019) study the two main types of digital platforms: transaction platforms and innovation platforms (Figure 4.1). The main purpose of the former is to facilitate transactions between different organizations, individuals, entities and to connect stakeholders. They can be understood as online marketplaces, offering the possibility for remote individuals or entities to share information, sell, buy or access a wide variety of services (Cusumano et al. 2019). Uber, Vinted or Airbnb are illustrations of transaction platforms that facilitate exchanges between buyers and sellers (of rides, second-hand clothing or overnight stays), and where the price mechanisms structure the transaction. The platform's business model is based on a paid commission. For example, in the case of LinkedIn, the platform brings together information providers and information seekers and the platform's business model is based on a subscription. We will return to this point in section 4.1.2. In turn, innovation platforms provide a basic technology to other companies that can add their own innovation components. This helps to increase the value to the system as a whole (Teece 2017). Innovation platforms have the particularity of being made up of technology blocks that the owner(s) and ecosystem partners can share to create new and complementary products and services (Cusumano et al. 2019, p. 18). For example, Microsoft Windows, Google Android and Apple IOS are exploration systems implemented in computers or smartphones that can be identified as innovation platforms. Indeed, the Windows operating system, for example, has provided a standard environment for a multitude of developers to propose software compatible with this environment, and thus has contributed to strengthening the adoption of the personal computer. Windows is, in this sense, a platform for innovation.

The most common digital platforms are most often transactional platforms, while integrating an innovation component as suggested by Gawer (2021)[4]. Also, the author[5] proposes a representation of digital platforms according to three categories (Figure 4.1). The overlap between the category of transaction platforms and that of innovation platforms contributes to a third category, entitled "hybrid company". It includes, in particular, the GAFA.

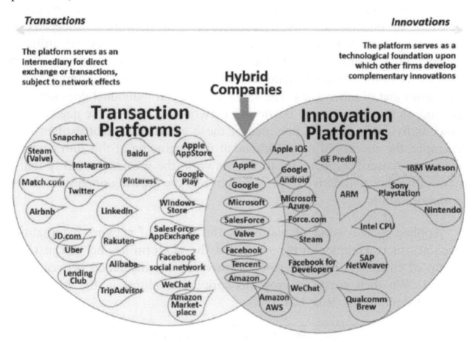

Figure 4.1. *Types of platforms (source: Gawer 2021). For a color version of this figure, see www.iste.co.uk/revest/digital.zip*

---

4 Some platforms can combine both forms, usually starting as a transaction platform and adding innovation components on an ongoing basis, so that the transactional platform becomes an innovation platform.

5 Based on research by Cusumano et al. (2019).

4.1.2. *Digital platform and a two-sided market*

The aim of a digital platform is to facilitate exchanges between dispersed groups of individuals. One of the crucial problems to be solved is that of connecting and coordinating individuals who do not know each other, the issue raised here being identical to that found in traditional markets. On a digital platform, the meeting of actors and their coordination are facilitated by the technology used (Iansiti and Levien 2004; Hautamäki and Oksanen 2018). Digital transaction platforms are particularly studied by the economic sciences, as they deal with the coordination of individuals, the market, price determination and contractual approaches. In particular, many studies (Box 4.1) have helped explain the success of platforms by the existence of network externalities. Developed in the 1980s (Katz and Shapiro 1985; Shapiro and Varian 1998), the notion of network externalities makes it possible to understand why a technology – a network – succeeds in developing and establishing itself. Through direct externalities, the utility of a technology increases when the number of its users increases. Each buyer/user in the market benefits not only from their own consumption but also from that of other users. The satisfaction of an individual does not only depend on their decision to buy/join a network but also on the decisions of other individuals. It is the presence of these externalities that explains, for example, the success of the telephone at the beginning of the 20th century: the more subscribers there are to the network, the greater the utility that a new subscriber will derive from it, because of the growing opportunities for communication.

Applied to the world of platforms, the notion of network externalities becomes more complex in the sense that the platform has not got just one group of customers but two, since it provides intermediation between two groups. We then speak of cross-network externalities in the context of two-sided platforms (Box 4.2).

> The work of Evans (2003) Rochet and Tirole (2003) gives platforms the characteristics of a two-sided market (also known as a multi-sided platform) whose objective is to facilitate exchanges between two groups of actors who would not have been able to meet or would have had difficulties in doing so. The externalities of networks play a central role in this context (Hagiu and Wright 2011) insofar as the platform's capacity to attract actors on one side also depends on its ability to do so on the other side. Blablacar is a perfect example of this situation. In order to attract potential trip buyers, the platform must also attract

potential trip providers. More generally, to increase the value of one side of the market and thus attract users to that side, the platform must demonstrate that it also attracts the other side of the market and vice versa.

Capturing these externalities is then crucial to success, and to do so, the platform must be able to reach a critical mass very quickly, i.e. a minimum number of participants on all sides necessary for its launch (Evans and Schmalensee 2017). Depending on the platform, this number varies and so do the strategies adopted to grow the sides. For example, to reach the critical mass, YouTube followed a zigzag strategy: the platform pushed participation from both sides (those uploading videos and those viewing them) but catering to one group more than another depending on the moment. Others have a two-step strategy (such as OpenTable, a restaurant reservation site in the United States): the platform starts persuading one side to participate and then the other. Finally, some platforms implement engagement strategies: a group needs to invest in order to participate. The members of this group need to have the guarantee that the other side will also participate. When Microsoft decided to enter the video game console market, it had to convince game developers that its future product Xbox would be a successful product. Microsoft's commitment to game developers was to guarantee that the product would be launched at a low price to ensure a viable and strong demand (Hagiu 2013).

Cross-network externalities are not the platform's only lever for action, and are closely linked to two other dimensions: price and the rules instituted by the platform. With regard to price, many intermediaries opt for an asymmetrical price (a paying side and a free side) between the two sides, which makes it possible to boost the dynamic only on one side, and helps to attract the other side (Roson 2005). Regarding the rules, the platforms establish a body of operating rules dedicated to the users of both sides, making it possible to frame the transaction[6]. By assuming the role of regulator (Boudreau and Hagiu 2009), the platform mobilizes a set of strategic instruments (legal, technological, informational) to organize the relationship.

Box 4.1. *Digital platforms, two-sided (or multi-sided) markets and cross-network externalities*

---

6 It should be noted that transaction platforms, such as Airbnb, secure transactions not only from a legal point of view but also through reputation control mechanisms (rating system, comments).

Thus, from an economic point of view, digital platforms are qualified as two-sided markets at the heart of which multiple externalities develop (Rochet and Tirole 2003; Gawer 2014; Evans and Schmalensee 2017). They facilitate exchanges by playing a match making role, and also by reducing the frictions that result from these same interactions.

As far as their remuneration model is concerned, they can charge fees to the parties who access the platform (by subscription or by access), they can also charge a commission as a percentage of the created for them or on a transaction, either to the seller (Vinted) or to the buyer (Blablacar) or both (eBay). But thanks to their two-sided market dimension, other methods of remuneration co-exist, in particular revenue from advertising or the monetization of user data. Table 4.1 summarizes different typical configurations of digital platforms in terms of price and revenue.

Platform	Paying side	Free side
PC operating system	PC users pay directly or indirectly via the PC manufacturer	Developers do not pay access fees to exploit the system's[7] APIs and pay only a nominal fee for the software development kit
E-commerce	Sellers often pay a commission	Buyers in general do not pay
Online job offers	Employers pay to advertise or recruit	Job seekers do not pay
Search engine	Companies pay for advertising	Internet users do not pay the search service

Table 4.1. *Paying side and free side: examples of two-sided activities (source: Evans and Schmalensee (2017))*

As we have just seen, the concepts of multi-sided markets and cross-network externalities provided by the economic sciences are indispensable for understanding the existence and characteristics of digital platforms. However, at the heart of digital platforms, real platform companies are actually exploiting (1) the reduction of transaction costs, which allows them to lower the costs of searching for information,

---

7 Application Programming Interface (API).

contracting and executing contracts; (2) the mechanism of disintermediation/re-intermediation, which allows these platform companies to destabilize the classic intermediaries, like what Uber does with taxis; (3) crowdsourcing, which allows the massive integration of the user into the value chain of the company platform, by mobilizing the lever of contribution and the aspiration to share; (4) algorithms that make it possible to exploit massive data; (5) the shift of services of an offer that was previously ensured by the acquisition of goods, such as the provision of self-service means of transport such as Vélov, Vélib or Dott; (6) the trusted third party that allows the company platform to have not only a role of intermediation but also of organizer of payments, based on the verification of identity, the rating system, as well as on user comments and opinions; (7) the valuation of depreciated assets when the platform, by reducing transaction costs, makes it possible to share, enhance or even make profitable, unused or depreciated purchased assets: platforms offering individuals and companies renting their car in a very simple way (Ouicar, Getaround, etc.) illustrates this trend.

The management sciences are valuable in showing how much the platforms offer companies, both commercial and non-commercial, the means to develop new strategies and new organizations. In this context, platforms are characterized by their ability to capture value, thanks to access to a multitude of customers to whom they can offer a variety of services while benefiting from increasing returns to scale. Far from being mere technical tools, digital platforms accompany the development of new business models, one of the main effects of which is to destabilize the historical players. Generally developed by start-ups seeking to penetrate sectors that are sometimes saturated, they contribute to building strategies that are then described as "disruptive" to indicate the way in which these start-ups are able to compete with established companies. But they can also serve the survival or development of small structures. This is the case of small video game studios that have managed to differentiate themselves from large publishers by developing a multi-sided platform that brings together groups of complementary users (Parmentier and Gandia 2016). However, this does not prevent the platforms from having purposes that are not always lucrative and from contributing to the growth of a sharing economy[8]. In addition to

8 Not to say a "collaborative economy" in order to avoid the ambiguity of the term (Vallat 2015, p. 5).

being a lever for new business models, management sciences show that platforms promote organizational innovations, allowing the companies concerned to be flexible in a more decentralized operation (Benavent 2016).

Beyond the transaction platforms, which are innovation platforms, and at the head of which we find true "platform companies" (Gawer 2021), there is another platform model that positions itself as an intermediary: the innovation intermediation platform. Its objective is to encourage and contribute to the development of innovation, as defined by the OECD, on the part of a diversity of actors, companies, associations and individuals. The specificity of these initiatives is that they are generated by public organizations and private companies.

4.2. From innovation intermediation platforms (IIPs) to public innovation intermediation platforms (PIIPs)

In this section, we focus on a specific category of digital platforms whose purpose is to foster the emergence of innovations in the economy. Often referred to as "crowdsourcing platforms", they can be characterized as "intermediation spaces" that put requesters and solution providers in contact with each other around questions related to the emergence of new knowledge, most often technological (Lakhani and Panetta 2007; Liotard and Revest 2018). To avoid confusing them with the innovation platforms analyzed above (such as Google), we will call them "innovation intermediation platforms" (IIPs).

The role of these IIPs is precisely to bring together companies faced with research and/or innovation problems (seekers), and Internet users from all over the world (solvers), becoming experts in a particular field who can provide a solution to the specific problems posed. Most often, IIPs organize online competitions, putting solvers in competition with each other based on a question (challenge), over a short period of time and with a prize (award). In this section, we expose the common points and the differences between two of these platforms: the private platform Innocentive and the public American platform platform Challenge.Gov. This perspective will then lead us to highlight the specificities of a public platform.

4.2.1. *Innocentive, a private intermediary innovation platform*

Created in 2000, Innocentive is a spin-off of Elly Lilly and is the oldest and best-known innovation platform[9]. There is a worldwide community of 500,000 *solvers,* registered free of charge, of different nationalities, and with diverse profiles (scientists, doctors, researchers, engineers, employees, retirees, consultants). The online challenges last from 30 to 60 days, with prizes ranging from $5,000 to $500,000 (some of them up to $1 million, the average being $20,000). The innovation themes are varied, including materials, chemistry, physics, life sciences, ecology, genetics, etc. The platform reports a challenge resolution rate of between 60 and 80%. Recent challenges have focused on questions related to Covid-19, while older challenges have aimed to find solutions to curb an oil spill or to develop new gloves for astronauts (a challenge initiated by NASA).

Innocentive attracts some 50 major companies and foundations (Solvay, Procter and Gamble, Boeing, DuPont, Novartis, IBM, Johnson & Johnson, Bayer, Syngenta, research foundations such as Rockefeller Foundation, Prize4Life). These companies are characterized by a sustained R&D strategy. The motivations of the seekers are multiple, even though the services and benefits invoiced by Innocentive can reach significant sums[10] (Liotard and Revest 2015). The seeker benefits from the intermediation offered by the platform, allowing them to benefit from the expertise of Internet users who do not belong to their own circle of acquaintances, and thus benefits from a wide range of skills. The system contributes to the acquisition of external knowledge by a company in a bottom-up movement, and to proposing an accelerated positive appropriation. For the company, this system leads to the collection of sometimes new knowledge, most often multidisciplinary.

The modularity of the question raised (a question fragmented into several sub-questions that will be the subject of particular challenges) increases the likelihood of success by reducing the scope of the research question, and ensures that the company remains anonymous to its competitors (Lakhani

---

9 https://www.innocentive.com/.

10 A study by Forrester (2009) shows that Syngenta, part of the seed industry, filed 14 challenges over three years for a total cost of about $5 million (including training, writing, support and administrative costs).

and Panetta 2007). The modularity also allows for a quicker response time, which can be a crucial strategic asset, and also makes it easier for internal R&D departments to take ownership of the solution(s) obtained. The interest of companies in these online competitions also lies in the short time between the beginning of the competition and the solution (about six to seven months).

Innocentive has the characteristics of a two-sided market. The three criteria of externalities, price and rules are clearly visible: (1) to develop cross-network externalities instead of cross-externalities, a major communication policy has been put in place, encouraging both groups to register on the platform. The main tools are the following: website and blog, diffusion of information on the challenges in different channels (relay via the sites of scientific journals, etc.), sponsorship or referral system between solvers, partnerships with universities; (2) the pricing policy is designed so that solvers can register for free in order to attract them, while the other side (the seekers) pays the fees charged by the intermediary; (3) the rules (legal, technological, informational) constitute one of the essential criteria for the proper functioning of the platform, in order to organize the relationship between the actors of the two markets as well as possible.

The originality and success of innovation intermediation platforms such as Innocentive are not only based on the potential offered by Web 2.0, but also on the nature of the intermediation implemented. In order to respond to the innovation problems of its clients, Innocentive has developed an adapted organizational mode, associated with an original business model (Table 4.2). First, intermediation is based on the rules of exchange at the heart of online competitions. Second, it is continuous, in the sense that the members of the platform supervise and control the progress of the operations on each side of the market from the moment the challenge is put online to its resolution. Third, intermediation is not only a connection between supply and demand, but it also influences each step of the relationship through different actions.

The innovation intermediation platform allows the different parties to be connected in the exchange. It also contributes to producing advice (training, challenge writing, solution selection) for clients, and develops a specific innovation method called Challenge Driven Innovation.

Finally, it participates in the evaluation of the challenges via the level of award. In this sense, it fulfills the functions of matchmaker, advisor and *evaluator* (Bessy and Chauvin 2013). The interactive and dynamic nature of Innocentive's intervention at the different stages mentioned, resulting in back and forth between the intermediary and the two sides of the market, also appears to be a preponderant property of the platform. Another property of this intermediation is the combination of human intermediation (the platform's employees) and non-human intermediation (the digital tools put in place: website, blog, project room). In the context of Innocentive, this combination has the particularity of making what was not marketable: the knowledge brought by the solution provider now has a value, even though sometimes they are not aware of its possible market transfer. All these elements constitute the core of the platform's business model.

4.2.2. Challenge.Gov, an innovation intermediary government platform

In the early 2010s, US federal Agencies expressed a strong interest in the use of digital platforms for platforms for innovation purposes. This phenomenon has led to institutional support for the Agencies in order to feed the public innovation support system in favor of innovation contests. The interest of the American public authorities in this type of scheme can be explained by the tighter public research context of recent years, characterized by the fall in public research budgets. However, through the contests, the research costs are borne by the competitors or teams. Moreover, unlike a traditional system of direct subsidies or research contracts, in which an agency finances ex ante results that may occur ex post (radical uncertainty), the competition makes it possible to reward for the result, only once it is known and selected (Kalil 2012). This externalization of a part of public research thus leads to placing part of the risk on companies and their competitors, and no longer on the Agency itself.

The configuration of intermediation on the Challenge.Gov website, created in 2010 and aimed at US Federal Agencies, resembles at first glance that of Innocentive since there is intermediation between two sides of the market (the Agencies and the Internet users). Among the many actors submitting competitions, four dominate: NASA, HHS (Health and Human Services), the Environmental Protection Agency and the US Air Force. The science and technology field is the most prominent, followed by health, energy and environment and education (Desouza and Mergel 2013). These contests are rewarded with both monetary and non-monetary awards. The highest monetary awards correspond to competitions where capital investment is high and the need for specialized knowledge is substantial (science and technology). Current awards range in size from $1,000 to $15 million. Non-monetary awards cover contests to provide information to the public, raise awareness of a particular issue or change certain behaviors (Mergel et al. 2014). These incentives can take the form of awards, medals, gifts, ceremonies, invitations and advertising.

The Challenge.Gov platform is managed by an organization: the General Services Administration (GSA) which provides upstream support to the Agencies. The competitions are visible on the platform, and are characterized by a summary and by links to dedicated websites. The associated monetary incentives are specified and the duration of the contest also. However, unlike Innocentive, the Agencies are clearly identified (no anonymity), and for many contests, the bonuses turn out to be non-monetary[11]. The target of Challenge.Gov is the citizen who can, individually or in teams, answer a challenge. Agencies are free to choose the source of funds if the incentive is monetary: either public or a combination of public and private. They can collaborate with each other to support a competition or partner with the private sector. They must set up committees of external experts (companies, another agency, universities, associations, etc.) that will help define the competition themes, or carry out the necessary evaluations, and provide technical assistance.

The design of the competition can vary: form of the competition, possibility of collaboration between competing teams or not. The criteria for selection and evaluation are also multifaceted. The policy of intellectual property rights is developed by each Agency, which decides on the way to deal with the transfer of rights. In this respect, IP management differs here from the Innocentive platform. Each Agency sets its own rules. Finally, participants in contests can be citizens, resident permanent Americans and economic actors (Master 2008; Brennan et al. 2012; Lakhani and Tong 2012).

---

11 For example, as part of the Stop Bullying video contest, students were invited to submit videos that "send a positive message to youth about the importance of being 'more than a bystander' to bullying in their schools and communities". Winners received gifts, not monetary awards.

	Innocentive.com	Challenge.Gov
Digital organization of the relationship	Consultation of challenges on www.innocentive.com Creation of a secure space to organize confidential exchange Consultation of a solvers' blog so that they can exchange with each other and read each other's experiences and testimonials	Consultation of challenges on www.challenge.gov Sites dedicated to the different competitions
Creation of value	Seekers: call upon external solution providers to solve challenges, benefitting from selection, ensure the transfer and development of solutions Solvers: transfer their technology, market the solution, make themselves known, get recruited	Seekers: receive solutions on technological and social issues, propose intellectual property clauses, raise awareness among different categories of citizens, communicate on societal issues (climate, environment, etc.) Solvers: propose solutions, form teams, create new businesses, make themselves visible
Internal organization and value chain implemented by the platform	Attracting solvers: communication via scientific journals and networks, partnerships with universities, sponsorship between solvers to attract others Assisting the seeker: management of the challenge (training, formalization and writing of the problem, breaking down of the question, setting of the premium), intellectual property clauses provided by Innocentive, filtering of the solutions by the platform and completion of the transaction	GSA manages the site, provides training (*webminar*) via the GSA platform (Digital.Gov), provides case studies, analyzes awards and competitions for the Community of Practice (CoP), made up of 730 federal Agency managers: the CoP meets quarterly, provides agencies with access to the solvers' community, offers technical expertise to agencies, a toolkit for developing competitions is made available
Value capture by the platform	Seekers pay fees to post a challenge, to train, they pay bonuses Solvers: no fees	Seekers: the use of the platform is free for the agencies, the costs supported by the agencies are the premiums paid in the framework of the competitions Solvers: no fee to participate in the challenges, but they can spend significant amounts of money to implement their solution
Market segment	Seekers: public and private companies, research foundations Solvers: students, researchers, scientists, employees, retirees, consultants	Seekers: all federal public and parapublic Agencies; defense, energy, education, NASA, etc. Solvers: American and international companies, citizens or certain categories (high school and university students)

Table 4.2. *Organization of intermediation at Innocentive.com and Challenge.Gov*

Thus, the intermediation of the Challenge.Gov platform, embodied by the GSA, seems less thorough than that of Innocentive. While the GSA acts as a matchmaker through services provided to the Agencies, it does not provide the functions of consultant and evaluator. Indeed, it is the Agencies, at the origin of the competitions who directly assume these last two functions. In this context, the functions of consultant and evaluator are exercised directly by the federal Agencies and respond to their concerns. In other words, the Agencies are responsible for drafting the challenges, determining the form and amount of the evaluation, and ensuring that the evaluation is conducted in a fair and transparent manner. They are influenced in these processes by their own motivations, the main objective being to encourage innovation in targeted areas. Challenge.Gov can then be considered as a "resource" platform for the Agencies, providing them with all the necessary help to post a competition, but not managing them in any way.

4.2.3. *First conceptualization of public innovation intermediation platforms (PIIPs)*

In this section, based on the two previous examples, we want to shed light on the particularities of public platforms designed to stimulate innovation, compared to private platforms. We call them public innovation intermediation platforms (PIIPs). They constitute new forms of political action, stimulating innovation thanks to digital tools. If they are part of an open innovation movement, as is the case for private platforms, they, however, have their own characteristics. In the remainder of this section, we consider only public innovation intermediation platforms (PIIPs) with contests (for other forms of PIIPs that will not be discussed in this chapter, see Box 4.2).

In general, the digital revolution has opened up the possibility for governments to transform the innovation processes for public services. More specifically, public sector organizations have seen the opportunity to move from a hierarchical internal innovation mode, to an innovation mode open to external stakeholders, and in particular to citizens. Thus, the latter can become actors in the improvement, design and delivery of public services (Felina and Zenger 2014). The participation of stakeholders external to the public sector has led in some cases to cooperation in the form of co-production of values. The latter can in turn take on several configurations: co-creation, co-design, co-implementation, co-delivery and co-evaluation (Mergel 2020). The degree of co-production can also vary according to the public policy instruments, and according to the will of the decision-makers. Public forms of open innovation (OI) generate innovations that can be classified into two main categories: innovations intended to directly improve public services (understood in the broadest sense) and innovations intended to provide new ideas and solutions in directions deemed by public actors to be crucial for the future – climate change, biodiversity protection, the effects of aging populations, medical desertification in certain areas, etc. In the second case, the themes solicited also depend on the type of public organization involved: international, national (governments) or regional.

In the framework of PIIPs, citizens who constitute the crowd by proposing solutions contribute their knowledge and expertise to respond to specific challenges launched by a public actor. In this sense, PIIPs are not far from their private counterparts (such as Innocentive) since they work within a crowdsourcing process[12]. The knowledge offered by citizens on PIIPs can take different forms, depending on the degree of expertise, while complex problems can be monodisciplinary or multidisciplinary. In the latter case, it can be a question of answering problems requiring the contribution of different disciplines, both scientific and non-scientific (see, for example, the European Portal of H2020 contests described in Chapter 1, which is an illustration of this).

The comparison between private and public platforms highlights three major differences that we detail.

The first difference concerns the type of innovation deployed on these platforms. The observation of the functioning of the platforms Challenge.Gov and Innocentive platforms tends to show that the concept of OI in the public sector differs, at least in part, from that applied to the private sector (Mergel 2015; Randhawa et al. 2019). Indeed, these public platforms do not necessarily seek to bring about radical innovations or new *business models* based on return on investment. They are more focused on incremental innovations, particularly in terms of improving the efficiency of

---

12 However, this public crowdsourcing is to be distinguished from real co-production activities of public services and products. Indeed, co-production involves a process in which citizens are real partners in the production of public value (Voorberg et al. 2015).

public services or raising awareness of certain themes not taken into account by the private sector and major global issues (climate, energy).

It is important to note that in parallel to the PIIPs with contests, there are other forms where innovation does not result from the outcome of a competition, but constitutes a collective or individual production of each Internet user, feeding the collective knowledge. It is more about contributions in terms of new ideas/knowledge than innovation. Some collaborative platforms are oriented towards initiatives that intend to facilitate citizenship through new technologies. For example, Fluicity, launched in 2019, is a citizen consultation platform that aims to pool ideas on all types of topics[13]. In 2018, Fluicity was ranked among the top GovTechs at the European summit organized by Public.io. The GovTech, brings together all technological solutions that enable the transformation and improvement of public services, supported by an ecosystem of entrepreneurs and start-ups.

At the same time, digital platforms oriented toward the open science movement have multiplied. Zooniverse[14] is the largest collaborative platform for the sciences of the universe. This platform has generated new scientific discoveries, the construction of databases useful to the scientific community and the publication of numerous research articles. For its part, NASA has launched several citizen science projects allowing 1 million volunteers from around the world to collaborate with scientists, notably in the collection of data on biodiversity, exploration of the sun, comets and planets outside the solar system (Nasa 2020).

Box 4.2. *Collaborative PIIPs: from the emergence of new ideas to open science*

The second difference lies in the expectations and objectives of the two categories of platforms. The main expectations of public organizations mobilizing digital and crowdsourcing platforms (Mergel 2015) are not only to get feedback on the quality of the public services offered, or even proposals for improvement from citizens, but also, in return, to inform, raise awareness and educate them on specific subjects. The aim here is to make people aware of the importance of certain societal issues, and to transform, if possible, behaviors in the desired direction. In the same way, as regards the provision of participants' knowledge to the contests, the aim is to obtain

---

13 https://get.fluicity/.
14 https://www.zooniverse.org/.

in-depth knowledge and real expertise on complex issues, and also to encourage the sharing of expertise. The study of the European portal of innovation competitions (Chapter 1 in this book) tends to show that public platforms represent an opportunity to bring together knowledge and experts from different scientific fields (biology, computer science, psychology, etc.), in order to respond to major global and complex challenges. In other words, the platforms would be a privileged "place" for interdisciplinarity, in order to encourage the sharing of knowledge from different scientific fields and to organize their interactions. This result leads us to consider the PIIPs as an operational lever for the development of responsible innovations. Indeed, these PIIPs can initiate and implement a so-called inclusive approach in the resolution of challenges. According to the responsible research and innovation approach, an inclusive approach makes it possible to better anticipate the impacts and risks of an innovation. Through the engagement and cooperation of civil society, it facilitates the alignment of innovations with society's values, needs and desires, and also helps to reduce the negative impacts of innovations through early involvement of all stakeholders (Gay et al. 2019).

A final key difference between these two types of platforms concerns the expected effects of crowdsourcing. In the private sector, the objectives take the form of creating new products/services, new markets, and the determinants are the expected performance and profitability of the companies involved. The PIIPs, on the contrary, mostly pursue economic (meso- or macro-economic) and/or societal objectives. The objectives take the form of job creation, local development, reduction of inequalities, increase of knowledge, etc.

Our reflection leads to a first definition of PIIPs: they are digital devices characterized by a public crowdsourcing. The main objective of these challenges is to have an eco-societal impact, either through a direct impact on citizens or indirectly by capturing knowledge and skills that can ultimately help address major contemporary challenges. The adoption and development of digital platforms by public organizations offer numerous prospects for improving and modernizing public action. In order to enlighten public decision-makers on the proper use of these PIIPs, we underline the importance of a multidisciplinary approach, combining economics, management and engineering sciences.

4.3. The contribution of engineering sciences to the analysis of PIIPs: some directions to explore

If economics is essential for understanding the mechanisms of market and non-market exchanges[15] of platforms, and if management sciences allow us to understand the platform as a new organizational form and as a lever for transforming business models, the engineering sciences offer a common perspective: considering the platform as a complex technical project, the design of which is a fundamental stage and the efficiency of which can be improved continuously, according to the needs of users.

In the engineering sciences, the innovation platform represents principally a physical or virtual "space" that combines several types of innovation activities and services (such as incubation, prototyping, coworking, forms of experimentation, etc.), the range of these services and activities corresponding to the platform's functionalities, which challenge the usage patterns and must respond to the needs of the users. Most of the time, therefore, these are innovation platforms as described in the first section. But they can also be platforms for innovation intermediation, as described in the second section, whose main objective is to contribute to the development of innovation through contests. In both cases, these platforms support an open innovation process whose design is specific.

As a product, regardless of its form, the platform is the subject of a design that constitutes the central object of engineering sciences (Oget 2018). In particular, the diversity of user profiles and the integration of all the tasks necessary to carry out an operational innovation process are two requirements to be considered from the first phases of designing an innovation platform. Thus, from this initial stage, the platform is considered as a product designed and developed according to specific standards, translating the various user needs into technical characteristics defined and formalized into specification. Also, in addition to economics and management sciences, engineering sciences consider the design phase of an innovation platform to be central, through the following questions: how are the users' profiles and needs integrated into the platform's design and development specifications? How does the design and development model

---

15 The use of platforms in the non-market economy corresponds, most of the time, to what is called the sharing economy, based on the sharing of objects and/or the production of collective knowledge. The Wikipedia platform is an emblematic example (Botsman and Rogers 2010).

chosen for the platform impact user behavior and consequently the lifespan of these platforms?

In order to answer these questions, we need to understand how the concept of innovation is integrated into the notion of digital platforms. Three directions are proposed here: the contributions of an approach in terms of process, the contributions of the open innovation platform approach and that of modularity and lifecycle.

4.3.1. *The contributions of a process approach*

One of the possible contributions of engineering sciences to the analysis of innovation platforms is the analysis in terms of process. A process is the modeling of a set of correlated or interacting operations or activities that use inputs to produce an expected result. The analysis in terms of process constitutes one of the foundations of the ISO standards, as a lever of a quality management system, allowing a continuous improvement approach, with regard to the satisfaction of customers and other stakeholders. In quality management systems, the process approach is defined as "a methodical approach to management, within the framework of which an organization identifies, monitors and manages its internal processes and their interactions"[16].

The process approach can be valuable in the design of open innovation intermediation platforms. Indeed, according to this approach, the quality of the product/service generated by an innovation depends strongly on the quality of the process used to develop and implement this innovation. The process itself is only as effective as the decisions taken in it. In the context of PIIPs with contest, the process approach is a way to control an element that is crucial to its success: the organizational architecture of the competition, i.e. the rules that define all the elements of the competition. This includes the rules defining all stages of the competition, from the eligibility of participants to the mode of rewarding winners, including the criteria for selecting the solution, the guidelines for a contest and the types of partnerships.

The efficiency of a process also depends on the speed with which the information needed for each decision is processed. Stage-gate frameworks

---

16 ISO 10014:2021(en), 3.6.

can help to ensure the quality of the process by forcing it to pass through checkpoints. These check points, defined ex ante, make it possible to better target the project thanks to lists of criteria and requirements specific to each phase, to minimize the risks, to ensure feedback of the process and the quality of its execution, to reduce the development time and finally to guarantee a project/product which meets the requirements of the customers. In the context of PIIPs with contest, this step-by-step evaluation approach makes it possible to envisage the operationalization of an RRI approach (Responsible Research and Innovation) which involves the implementation of an innovation process anticipatory, reflective, deliberative and reactive (Gay et al. 2019).

Considering PIIPs as an open innovation design process, collaboration and connection with the outside world also appear as two major aspects of the platform's functioning. It is then appropriate to consider the main functions of an open innovation process whose functionalities are diverse and complex. In the design engineering phase, all of these functionalities are described as technical requirements in a specification with two main issues: an open innovation platform must be an interface and a real collaboration space.

4.3.2. The Open Innovation Platform (OIP): from a characterization in technical terms

The use of IT-based tools is constitutive of open innovation. From his first book, Chesbrough (2006) emphasizes the importance of IT tools for open innovation. In the engineering sciences, an OIP is initially thought of as a product platform composed of a set of sub-systems and interfaces that form a common and complex structure from which a flow of derived products or services can be developed and produced efficiently (Meyer and Lehnerd 1997). With the development of digital tools, innovation platforms are seen as virtual environments that serve as infrastructures for information exchange (Gayoso et al. 2017)[17]. Indeed, they provide an interface that allows users (or innovators) to interact with the platform without the limits of time or place.

From a technical point of view, the platform is the supporting product that provides an informational infrastructure that guides organizations towards open and distributed innovation models. In its essentials, a platform

---

17 This refers to innovation platforms innovation platforms in the terminology of Cusumano et al. (2019), described in section 4.1.

provides a common base and a place where a wide range of entities can converge to create and deliver value. Connection to an OIP is possible via APIs (Application Programming Interface). These applications allow an automatic connection to the platform in order to exchange information or access services (Linagora 2017). They allow computer programs developed by the partners to connect to the platform. There are closed APIs, restricted to a specific group of users, and open APIs, accessible to all, constituting a platform based on an open approach, especially public platforms. It is therefore an essential technological brick that allows an organization not only to appeal to the crowd but also to build an ecosystem of partners.

The range of services offered by the platform can be expanded by the modularity of its architecture, allowing it to respond to the diverse demands of customers in terms of innovation. Thinking of the OIP as a product platform thus makes it possible to envisage its evolution, from design to service delivery, supported by a modular vision.

4.3.3. ... to a vision in terms of modularity and lifecycle

Modular architectures for the design and development of complex products are widely discussed in the scientific literature (e.g. Subbu et al. 1999). Modular design, which consists of decomposing a product into more or less independent elements, is of interest not only for reducing design time, but also for reducing costs and product complexity. Initially conceived from a technical point of view, the modular approach has gradually been extended to the organization: "The modularity of products tends to favor the modularity of the organization that manufactures and designs these products" (Cohendet et al. 2005, p. 122). Also, following Herbert Simon and under the influence of Sanchez and Mahoney (1996), modularity itself becomes a specific organizational structure, with qualities of coordination and division of labor, which is based, in particular, on the development of a complete information structure.

The concept of modularity is particularly well suited to innovation platforms that allow for the production of products/services that permit functional variations. A modular technology architecture involves a stable, shared set of components (Baldwin and Clark 2000), assembled into three categories (Tiwana et al. 2010): the core, interfaces and complementary modules, which increase the functionality of the core (Baldwin and

Woodward 2009). Modularity should be applied not only in the development phase, but also at different stages of the lifecycle.

Research on modular architectures tends to show that they facilitate innovation by making it easier to manage complexity (Simon 1962; Parnas 1972; Langlois and Robertson 1992; Baldwin and Clark 2000; Schilling 2000; Langlois 2002). Indeed, thanks to modularity, each module becomes autonomous, allows for innovation, which is also autonomous, and facilitates innovative recombinations of modules (Garud and Kumaraswamy 1995). The platform engineering approach considers platforms as technological architectures with physical interfaces configured to facilitate innovation. A modular architecture must specify which modules will be part of the system and what their functions will be. The interfaces describe in detail how the modules complement each other, communicate and interact (Baldwin and Clark 2000, p. 63).

Nevertheless, modular architectures are difficult to develop and questions arise about the transformation capabilities of the core architecture as well as the degree of openness interfaces (West 2007)[18].

In this context, Product Lifecycle Management (PLM) systems provide a framework for managing the operational complexity of modular design activities. If PLM systems are applied to product lifecycles in the industry, they can be mobilized to enrich our understanding of digital platforms. Because of the characteristics of open innovation, an OIP should not be thought of as a monolithic product or even as an assembly of separately designed components. The application of the PLM approach leads us to think of OIPs as an architecture, a "system of systems". More precisely, it leads us to think of OIPs as an open structuring tool, which enables mediation between the actors involved and serves as a support for their transactions in a systemic logic.

---

18 Recently, Gawer (2021) has proposed an analysis of the boundaries of digital firms/platforms, which integrates approaches from economics, strategic management and information systems. These boundaries are understood *through* three dimensions: (1) the scope of the platform (who owns the assets? what activities are performed?), (2) the configuration and composition of the platform's faces (which groups of customers have access to the platform?) and (3) the digital interfaces (how are data exchanged between the platform and each of the faces involved?).

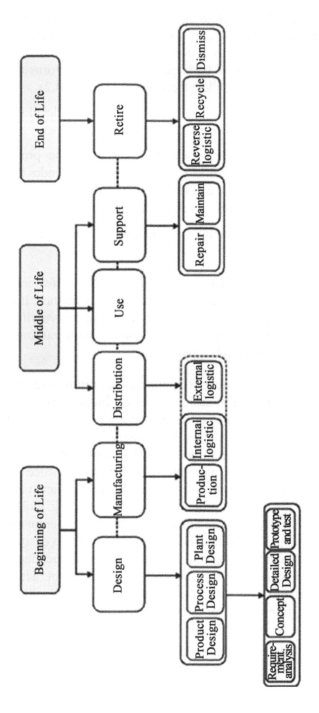

Figure 4.2. *The product lifecycle model (source: Terzi et al. 2011). For a color version of this figure, see www.iste.co.uk/revest/digital.zip*

The PLM model[19] is used to manage products through all phases of the lifecycle "from cradle to grave" (Terzi et al. 2011). While reference to the "lifecycle model" leads to different characterizations, in general, the "product lifecycle" consists of three phases in which information must be managed and tracked, and knowledge capitalized (Figure 4.2):

– The early life phase includes all phases of product development, from concept definition to production and delivery to the customer.

– The mid-life phase includes mainly the use of the product by the customer, and possibly maintenance and repair. It also includes the evolution and upgrading of components (e.g. replacing a sensor with a more accurate one) or the updating of software or related applications.

– The end-of-life phase includes disassembly, reuse, refurbishment or recycling of the product.

The PLM approach, in the context of a platform for innovation, is designed to integrate, streamline and improve its performance. It is presented as a system in which all stakeholders are involved in an evolving logic. The aim is to accommodate a wide variety of content with varying degrees of structure in a "collaborative hub" approach.

PLM appears to be the most efficient tool to rationalize the collective contributions to the platform design process. Indeed, as an information system, PLM facilitates the virtual coexistence of physically distant actors around this design process. Mainly in industry, Cina (2017) extends this thinking and asks the question of whether platforms in general and PLM in particular "should be used in every phase of the design process in order to bring about innovation, or whether it is preferable to use them only in certain key stages, given that they represent 'closed' structuring tools when they coordinate ecosystems and respond above all to the dominant logics of companies" (Cina 2017). For this, the author identifies two design processes. The distributed design process that manages the interdependence temporal between tasks. The stakeholders of the project do not act jointly but simultaneously in order to solve the problem collectively. PLM seems to offer a promising framework for the distributed design process. The second

19 One of the definitions of PLM allows us to appreciate how it is a cross-cutting and plural notion of a "holistic" type, bringing together "products, services, activities, process, people, skills, IT systems, data, knowledge, techniques, practices, procedures and standards" (Terzi et al. 2011; Stark 2014).

process is a co-design process, where the stakeholders must develop jointly with a temporal and cognitive interdependence. However, in this framework, where the issue is all in a cognitive synchronization, the PLM approach may find its limits (Cina 2017).

The PLM perspective seems not sufficient to understand the development of platforms lop without addressing the concept of ALM (Application Lifecycle Management). PLM concerns the hardware lifecycle of a product, while ALM concerns the software lifecycle. The objective of ALM is to provide a solution "to monitor, control and manage software development throughout the entire application lifecycle" (Deuter and Imort 2020, p. 234).

More specifically, there are two main stages: the design stage and the ALM stage. In the first stage, the requirements are grouped together, design and construction, which are at the heart of the creation of an application. The requirements are translated into functionalities in relation with the needs of management, interface, use and service. These requirements are transformed into specifications (design phase). In the design phase, the software and its architecture are developed and tests are performed. The second major stage, management stage, refers to the deployment, exploitation and optimization phases of the software lifecycle. Once the system is built, the deployment phase begins. During the exploitation phase, support must be provided to users and changes must be captured. The final phase of the ALM cycle is optimization: during this phase, the results of the operations conducted are analyzed. Therefore, feedback must be collected from the users.

The integration of the two PLM/ALM approaches appears to be an advantage for meeting the development needs of platforms that include more and more physical components and computer software. Over the last few years, industry and universities have developed several PLM/ALM integration concepts in order to ensure an efficient lifecycle management of smart and complex products in all domains (Deuter and Imort 2020).

4.4. Discussion and conclusion

The purpose of the discussion is to compare the analysis of the PIIPs proposed by the economics and management sciences with that of the digital innovation platforms proposed by the engineering sciences. Our hypothesis is that the technical analysis carried out by the engineering sciences can contribute to enriching the concept of innovation intermediary government platforms, and more generally that of public platforms. To do so, we review the main characteristics of PIIPs emerging from research in economics and management sciences. Then, we confront them with the engineering sciences.

As we pointed out in the first section of this chapter, while the concept of a private digital platform is at the heart of an important literature, the more recent concept of public platforms, which is more recent, has received less attention so far (Kankanhalli et al. 2017). The main characteristics of PIIPs according to economics and management science can be summarized as follows:

– PPIIs provide an opportunity for stakeholders in general and citizens in particular to participate in the public system by potentially acting at the different levels of designing, improving and delivering public services through five channels: co-creation, co-design, co-implementation, co-delivery and co-evaluation (Mergel 2020).

– Unlike private platforms, public platforms do not necessarily work to set up a new product/service, but reveal broader objectives (awareness of specific themes, improvement of public service, societal objectives, search for expertise on major technological issues, etc.), whose mode of action is based on crowdsourcing. The PIIP studied (Challenge.Gov) attests to this.

– The search for interdisciplinarity and the articulation of points of view from various disciplines are a fundamental challenge for the PIIPs in order to respond to major challenges, both societal and technological.

This first characterization could, according to us, be enriched thanks to the approach of digital platforms proposed by the engineering sciences. We wish to insist on the following differences and common points:

– Overall, economic and management approaches analyze platforms from an organizational and managerial point of view, while engineering science approaches focus on technical aspects. More precisely, economics and management sciences, on the one hand, and engineering sciences, on the other hand, are positioned at two complementary levels of analysis: the first will study the service offered and the conditions of its supply (the content) while the latter will focus on studying the technical support necessary for the deployment of the service – the contest – embodied here by the digital platform. Thus, PIIPs establish operating rules (of the contest if the latter is the form adopted) which we presented in the first section of this chapter, but these rules are to be distinguished from the technical rules of the platform.

– Another difference concerns the notion of platform design and the importance given to this phase. In economics and management, the design phase refers to the development of both the subject and the specific organizational context. For example, the study in the first section of this chapter of the PIIP, Challenge.Gov (and also the European platform in Chapter 1) reveals rules specific to the contests launched (and therefore to the service provided): rules for participation, rules for submitting the solution, rules for evaluation and rules for co-construction if necessary. However, the implementation of this type of rules relies on a base of other rules, in a way, anterior to the first ones, which we call "technical" rules established at the time of the platform's design. Indeed, the needs in terms of use and interfaces must be clearly expressed (what do we want?), the requirements must be translated technically through specification and programming actions, in order to build the architecture of the platform, which also includes the testing and correction phases. Thus, if the design phase is not correctly defined ex ante, there is a great risk that needs that may arise later in the operation of the platform and the provision of the service can no longer be taken into account, since the basic architecture cannot be modified or only with difficulty. The design phase is particularly crucial with regard to the "openness" dimension and inclusiveness of the stakeholders to the process. Indeed, it allows the articulation of the roles of the different stakeholders to be defined by their capacity and modality to interact with each other.

– The dynamic vision of the functioning of a digital platform is one of the strengths of engineering science approaches. Indeed, the ability of the platform to evolve is a crucial factor in order to allow the development of the platform in response to expectations and needs that are constantly changing. Although PLM and ALM models were not initially designed for the public sector, they have the potential to be adapted to platforms designed and managed by public actors. For example, the economic and management sciences are specifically interested in the management phase which includes the deployment/function/optimization stages, while the engineering sciences also include the design phase (requirement/design/construction). An ALM approach can integrate all these stages. The notion of product is perceived at different scales. The economic and management approaches consider the notion of product as the final result of the process (the contest as a service), while engineering sciences apprehend the platform as a product in itself (notion of platform-product). The same is true for the notion of modularity. It is an essential condition in the structural implementation of the platform from the point of view of the design. However, it does not always appear to be a necessity in the context of service delivery: only the case study of Innocentive.com has revealed its use when it comes to fragmenting the challenge. Indeed, in order to preserve the anonymity of the *seeker*, the platform's services help the latter to fragment the question asked so that competitors and other involved parties are not able to identify them.

– Finally, with regard to the role of users, the approaches seem to be similar. The user has an important role in the system and can be involved both in the design of the platform (engineering science) and in the provision of the service (during the various stages of the competition – economic and management sciences).

The two types of vision are summarized in Table 4.3.

	Economic and management science vision	**Engineering science vision**
Product	The service	The platform, the foundation of a service, is a product in itself
Rules	Rules of operation/delivery of the service (contest)	Lifecycle rules of the platform
Platform	Organization, operation within the service, management	Design/specifications/requirements but also uses
Vocabulary	Service/management	Architecture/module/interface/API/modularity
User	Yes	Yes (co-initiation with the user)/uses

Table 4.3. *Two visions to characterize a platform*

The objective of this chapter was to propose a first rapprochement of approaches in social sciences (particularly in economics and management) and in engineering sciences in order to better conceptualize the development, operation and transformation of a digital platform. For this, we relied on recent work in economics and management on public innovation intermediation platforms. If the research carried out in the private sector has made it easier for public actors to approach the notion of digital platform, there are still strong differences concerning the objectives and constraints in these two spheres (private and public). Gradually, studies analyzing public innovation intermediation platforms, such as Challenge.Gov in the United States, have highlighted the specificities of a public platform. However, a better understanding and representation of the latter could be provided by the contributions of engineering sciences, emphasizing the crucial role of (1) the technical dimension, notably through the notion of modularity; (2) the design phase and (3) the evolutive dimension through analyzes in terms of lifecycle, in particular the integration of PLM and ALM systems. If public decision-makers wish to pursue the reforms initiated concerning public actions and policies, oriented towards greater inclusiveness of stakeholders, open innovation, the integration of knowledge produced in several disciplinary fields during the construction of digital platforms appears to be a relevant and promising path to follow.

4.5. Acknowledgments

We would like to warmly thank Philippe Barbet for his careful review of this chapter. The research leading to this chapter was also supported by the European Union's Horizon 2020 research and innovation program under grant agreement No. 822781 GROWINPRO – Growth Welfare Innovation Productivity.

Chapter 4 has a special status because it is the product of many discussions and interactions with our colleagues in engineering and information sciences. It owes its existence to Aicha Sekhari and Jannik Laval of the DISP laboratory (Université Lumière Lyon 2), whom we sincerely thank for having opened our horizon on these disciplines, and enlightening us on the possibilities of bringing together the social sciences and the engineering sciences.

4.6. References

Baldwin, C.Y. and Clark, K.B. (2000). *Design Rules: The Power of Modularity*, Volume 1. MIT Press, Cambridge.

Baldwin, C.Y. and Woodard, J.J. (2009). The architecture of platforms: A unified view. In *Platforms, Markets and Innovation*, Gawer, A. (ed.). Edward Elgar, Cheltenham.

Benavent, C. (2016). *Plateformes*. FYP Éditions, Limoges.

Bessy, C. and Chauvin, P.M. (2013). The power of market intermediaries: From information to valuation processes. *Valuation Studies*, 1(1), 83–117.

Botsman, R. and Rogers, R. (2010). *What's Mine is Yours: The Rise of Collaborative Consumption*. HarperCollins, New York.

Boudreau, K. and Hagiu, A. (2009). Platform rules: Multi-sided platforms as regulators. In *Platforms, Markets and Innovation*, Gawer, A. (ed.). Edward Elgar, Cheltenham.

Brennan, T., Macauley, M., Whitefoot, K. (2012). Prizes, patents and technology procurement: A proposed analytical framework. Discussion Paper, Resources for the future, 11–21 [Online]. Available at: www.rff.org.

Chesbrough, H. (2006). Open innovation: A new paradigm for understanding industrial innovation. In *Open Innovation, Researching a New Paradigm*, Chesbrough, H., Vanhaverbeke, W., West, J. (eds). Oxford University Press, Oxford.

Chevallier, J. (2018). Vers l'État-plateforme ? *Revue française d'administration publique*, 3(167), 627–637.

Cina, M. (2017). Les nouvelles plateformes de conception, le PLM et leurs implications dans le processus de conception : portées et limites. *Gestion et management* [Online]. Available at: https://dumas.ccsd.cnrs.fr/dumas-01664212/document.

Cohendet, P., Diani, M., Lerch, C. (2005). Stratégie modulaire dans la conception. Une interprétation en termes de communautés. *Revue française de gestion*, 2005/5(158), 121–143.

Constantinides, P., Henfridsson, O., Parker, G.G. (2018). Introduction – Platforms and infrastructures in the digital age. *Information Systems Research*, 29(2), 381–400.

Cusumano, M.A., Gawer, A., Yoffie, D.B. (2019). *The Business of Platforms. Strategy in the Age of Digital Competition, Innovation, and Power*. HarperCollins, New York.

Desouza, K. and Mergel, I. (2013). Implementing open innovation in the public sector: The case of Challenge.Gov. *Public Administration Review*, 73(6), 882–890.

Deuter, A. and Imort, S. (2020). PLM/ALM Integration with the asset administration shell. In *5th International Conference on System-Integrated Intelligence*, Procedia Manufacturing, Lemgo, 234–240.

Evans, D. (2003). Some empirical aspects of multi-sided platform industries. *Review of Network Economics*, 2(3), 191–209.

Evans, P.C. and Gawer, A. (2016). The rise of the platform enterprise: A global survey. Working document, University of Surrey, The Emerging Platform Economy Series N°1, The Center for Global Enterprise.

Evans, D. and Schmalensee, R. (2017). *De précieux intermédiaires : comment Blablacar, Facebook, Paypal ou Uber créent de la valeur*. Odile Jacob, Paris.

Felina, T. and Zenger, T.R. (2014). Closed or open innovation? Problem solving and the governance choice. *Research Policy*, 43(5), 914–925.

Garud, R. and Kumaraswamy, A. (1995). Technological and organizational designs to achieve economies of substitution. *Strategic Management Journal*, 16(S1), 93–109.

Gawer, A. (2009). Platform dynamics and strategies: From products to services. In *Platforms, Markets and Innovation*, Gawer, A. (ed.). Edward Elgar Publishing, Cheltenham.

Gawer, A. (2014). Bridging differing perspectives on technological platforms: Toward an integrative framework. *Research Policy*, 43(7), 1239–1249.

Gawer, A. (2021). Digital platforms' boundaries: The interplay of firm scope, platform sides, and digital interfaces. *Long Range Planning*, 54(5), 102045.

Gay, C., Liotard, I., Revest, V. (2019). Les concours d'innovation en ligne : un instrument pertinent pour la recherche et l'innovation responsable. *Innovations*, 2(59), 129–150.

Gayoso, E., Jammet, T., Klein, N. (2017). Les plateformes d'innovation, de marque, de conseil. Vers une infrastructure numérique de la relation-client ? In *Les métamorphoses des infrastructures, entre béton et numérique*, Chatzis, K., Jeannot, G., November, V., Ughetto, P. (eds). Peter Lang, Brussels.

Hagiu, A. and Wright, J. (2011). Multi-sided platforms. *Harvard Business School Working Paper*, 12–024.

Hautamäki, A. and Oksanen, K. (2018). Digital platforms for restructuring the public sector. In *Collaborative Value Co-creation in the Platform Economy*, Smedlund, A., Lindblom, A., Mitronen, L. (eds). Springer, Singapore.

Hein, A., Schreieck, M., Riasanow, T., Setzke, D.S., Wiesche, M., Böhm, M., Krcmar, H. (2020). Digital platform ecosystems. *Electronic Markets*, 30(1), 87–98.

Iansiti, M. and Levien, R. (2004). *The Keystone Advantage. What the New Dynamics of Business Ecosystems Mean for Strategy, Innovation, and Sustainability*. Harvard Business School Press, Boston.

Kalil, T. (2012). The grand challenges of the 21st century [Online]. Available at: https://obamawhitehouse.archives.gov/sites/default/files/microsites/ostp/grandch allenges-speech-04122012-rev.pdf.

Kankanhalli, A., Zuiderwijk, A., Tayi, G.K. (2017). Open innovation in the public sector: A research agenda. *Government Information Quarterly*, 34(1), 84–89.

Katz, M.L. and Shapiro, C. (1985). Network externalities, competition, and compatibility. *The American Economic Review*, 75(3), 424–440.

Koskinen, K., Bonina, C., Eaton, B. (2019). Digital platforms in the global south: Foundations and research agenda. In *International Conference on Social Implications of Computers in Developing Countries*. Springer, Cham, 319–330.

Lakhani, K.R. and Panetta, J.A. (2007). The principles of distributed innovation. *Innovations: Technology, Governance, Globalization*, 2(3), 97–112.

Lakhani, K.R. and Tong, R. (2012). Public–private partnerships for organizing and executing prize-based competitions, WP n°2012-13. Berkman Center for Internet & Society at Harvard University.

Langlois, R.N. (2002). Modularity in technology and organization. *Journal of Economic Behavior & Organization*, 49(1), 19–37.

Langlois, R.N. and Robertson, P. (1992). Networks and innovation in a modular system: Lessons from the microcomputer and stereo component industries. *Research Policy*, 21(4), 297–313.

Linagora (2017). Les plateformes digitales au cœur de la transformation des organisations. Open source Pro [Online]. Available at: https://blog.linagora.com/wp-content/uploads/2017/06/Linagora-Livre-blanc-Open-Source-Pro-2017.pdf.

Liotard, I. and Revest, V. (2015). Le renouveau des concours aux États-Unis, dispositifs publics de stimulation à l'innovation complémentaires aux brevets. *Revue d'économie industrielle*, 253, 91–122.

Liotard, I. and Revest, V. (2018). Contests as innovation policy instruments: Lessons from the US federal agencies' experience. *Technological Forecasting and Social Change*, 127, 57–69.

Lusch, R.F. and Nambisan, S. (2015). Service innovation: A service-dominant logic perspective. *MIS Quarterly*, 39(1), 155–175.

Master, W. (2008). Accelerating innovation with prize rewards: A history and typology of prize contexts with motivation for a new contest design. *ifpri discussion paper 00835.*

Mergel, I. (2015). Opening government: Designing open innovation processes to collaborate with external problem solvers. *Social Science Computer Review*, 33(5), 599–612.

Mergel, I. (2020). La co-création de valeur publique par les directions du numérique : une comparaison internationale. *Action publique, recherche et pratique*, 6, 6–16.

Mergel, I., Bretschneider, S., Louis, C., Smith, J. (2014). The challenges of Challenge.Gov: Adopting private sector business innovations in the Federal Government. In *47th Hawaii International Conference on System Science*. IEEE Computer Society, 2073–2082.

Mergel, I., Edelmann, N., Haug, N. (2019). Defining digital transformation: Results from expert interviews. *Government Information Quarterly*, 36(4), 101385.

Meyer, M.H. and Lehnerd, A.P. (1997). *The Power of Product Platforms: Building Value and Cost Leadership*. The Free Press, New York.

NASA (2020). Open innovation at NASA: Enhancing problem solving and discovery through prize competitions, challenges, crowdsourcing, and citizen sourcing [Online]. Available at: https://www.nasa.gov/sites/default/files/atoms/files/2019_nasa_open_innovation_report_final.pdf.

Oget, D. (2018). La formation à la conception, entre sciences humaines et sciences de l'ingénieur. In *Les temps heureux des apprentissages*, Maubant, P. (ed.). Champ social, Nîmes.

Parmentier, G. and Gandia, R. (2016). Gérer l'ouverture dans un business model multiface : le cas du jeu vidéo en ligne. *Revue française de gestion*, 254(1), 107–128.

Parnas, D.L. (1972). On the criteria to be used in decomposing systems into modules. *Communications of the ACM*, 15(12), 1053–1058.

Randhawa, K., Wilden, R., West, J. (2019). Crowdsourcing without profit: The role of the seeker in open social innovation. *R&D Management*, 49(3), 298–317.

de Reuver, M., Sørensen, C., Basole, R.C. (2018). The digital platform: A research agenda. *Journal of Information Technology*, 33(2), 124–135.

Robert, C. (2019). L'introuvable intérêt général européen. L'essoufflement d'un mode de légitimation et ses enjeux. In *Au nom de l'intérêt général*, Gaboriaux, C. and Kaluszynski, M. (eds). Peter Lang, Brussels.

Rochet, J.C. and Tirole, J. (2003). Platform competition in two-sided markets. *Journal of the European Economic Association*, 1(4), 990–1029.

Roson, R. (2005). Two-sided markets: A tentative survey. *Review of Network Economics*, 4(2), 142–160.

Sanchez, R. and Mahoney, J. (1996). Modularity, flexibility, and knowledge management. In *Product and Organization Design. Strategic Management Journal*, 17, 63–76.

Schilling, M.A. (2000). Towards a general modular system theory and its application to interfirm product modularity. *Academy of Management Review*, 25(2), 312–334.

Shapiro, C. and Varian, H.R. (1998). *Information Rules: A Strategic Guide to the Network Economy*. Harvard Business Press, Brighton.

Simon, H.A. (1962). The architecture of complexity. *Proceedings of the American Philosophical Society*, 106(6), 467–482.

Stark, J. (2014). *Product Lifecycle Management: 21st Century Paradigm for Product Realisatio*, Volume 1. Springer, New York.

Subbu, R., Sanderson, A.C., Hocaoglu, C., Graves, R.J. (1999). Evolutionary decision support for distributed virtual design in modular product manufacturing. *Production Planning and Control*, 10(7), 627–642.

Teece, D.J. (2017). Dynamic capabilities and (digital). platform lifecycles. In *Entrepreneurship, Innovation, and Platforms*, Furman, J., Gawer, A., Silverman, B.S., Stern, S. (eds). Emerald Publishing Limited, Bingley.

Terzi, S., Bourras, A., Dutta, D., Garetti, M., Kiritsis, D. (2011). Product lifecycle management – From its history to its new role. *International Journal of Product Lifecycle Management*, 4(4), 360–389.

Tiwana, A., Konsynski, B., Bush, A. (2010). Research commentary – Platform evolution: Co-evolution of platform architecture, governance and environmental dynamics. *Information Systems Research*, 21(4), 675–687.

Toffler, A. (1980). *The Third Wave*. William Morrow, New York.

Vallat, D. (2015). Une alternative au dualisme État-Marché : l'économie collaborative, questions pratiques et épistémologiques. Working Paper du laboratoire Triangle WP01-12/15 [Online]. Available at: https://halshs.archives-ouvertes.fr/halshs-01249308.

Von Hippel, E. (1986). Lead users: A source of novel product concepts. *Management Science*, 32(7), 791–805.

Voorberg, W.H., Bekkers, V.J., Tummers, L.G. (2015). A systematic review of co-creation and co-production: Embarking on the social innovation journey. *Public Management Review*, 17(9), 1333–1357.

West, J. and O'Mahony, S. (2008). The role of participation architecture in growing sponsored open source communities. *Industry and Innovation*, 15(2), 145–168.

Conclusion

The main objective of this book was to study public policies and how the use of digital tools affects them by raising several questions: are public actors increasingly mobilizing these tools? What are the instruments/ mechanisms chosen? Do the categories of digital tools used influence the objectives and implementation of public policies? If so, in what way(s)?

While it is impossible to provide exhaustive answers to these questions, given the variety of both the policies conducted and the instruments or combinations of digital instruments that can be used, we have chosen to shed light on this issue through three illustrations: digital platforms and innovation policies, microsimulation models and social policies, and Big Data and health policies. Each of them highlights the effects of digitalization on public actions and policies.

Digital tools and public policies: towards increased integration… but not without difficulties

The study areas have enabled us to highlight several lessons. First, there is no single answer to the questions posed, and the specificity of the policies conducted in particular fields requires adapted tools, reflecting the objectives of the policy concerned, its challenges and its obstacles. For example, the case of Open Data and health policy raises crucial issues of ownership: who owns the data? Who can use it – researchers, practitioners, patients, companies? And for what type of use?

Conclusion written by Paul COTTON, Isabelle LIOTARD and Valérie REVEST.

Second, beyond the specificities linked to the themes chosen for public action, points of convergence emerge:

– in all the cases studied, digitization represents more than just the use of a new instrument. It tends to affect the very nature of the policies conducted. In other words, it induces a reflection on the design and implementation of these policies, highlighting the need for a more reflective approach;

– another common thread refers to the growing importance of the inclusion of stakeholders in the processes of policy design and implementation. The latter follow less and less a strict top-down process, and bring out more or less accentuated bottom-up forms of interaction;

– the relationship between political decision-makers and users or citizens is questioned and can sometimes be challenged;

– the need to understand the impact of policy measures on societal dynamics seems to be increasing, both in terms of process and purpose.

Elements relating to the use of data (ownership attributes in particular) and to the types of use (through governance) feed a questioning process that is becoming denser over time, and that the various actors involved will have to integrate into their analyses and decision-making processes. In addition to the concluding elements outlined above, we believe that future research should include other analyses in line with those we have conducted. In the next section, we propose opening three avenues of research in this area. On the one hand, as public decision-makers are increasingly confronted with global, interdisciplinary challenges, known as "grand challenges", can digitalization facilitate the management of these challenges? On the other hand, technological innovations have led to the appearance of other forms of interactions that will develop in the future, such as the citizen science movement or the use of artificial intelligence (AI). Finally, we have not directly addressed the issue of public policy evaluation. If the latter already appears to be complex and its treatment controversial, the effect of the digitalization of processes is likely to accentuate its complexity.

How to face major societal challenges

A current problem for public policies is that they are faced with increasingly complex challenges that include a societal dimension. Public decision-makers are trying to formulate appropriate responses to major societal issues such as global warming, the preservation of biodiversity or the aging of the population (Lindner et al. 2016). Thus, during the last H2020 program, the European Union highlighted six "grand challenges" at the heart of its concerns, including *Health, Demographic Change and Wellbeing*; *Food Security, Sustainable Agriculture*. The notion of "grand challenges", present not only in Europe but also in the United States, is not new (Hicks 2016; Kaldewey 2018). While for some scholars it refers to the emergence of a new paradigm in science, technology and innovation policy studies, for others it is merely the "recycling" of already existing concepts (Cagnin et al. 2012; Foray et al. 2012; Kallerud et al. 2013; Kuhlmann and Rip 2014; Ulnicane 2016). Nowadays, the majority of researchers converge on the argument that the very nature of societal grand challenges disrupts traditional public policy approaches. First, these grand challenges have too high a degree of complexity to be addressed through "command and control" mechanisms (Kuhlmann and Rip 2018). Grand challenges do not only concern scientific, technological themes, but they also include social concerns, with a particular focus on current issues of social innovation (Van Der Have 2016; Lukesch 2020). More generally, they are made up of heterogeneous elements and forces – beyond the distinction between social and technological components, which need to be identified, mobilized and integrated into new forms of public policy (Kuhlmann et al. 2014, 2018). Second, grand challenges are also characterized by a high degree of uncertainty and prove to be extremely fluid. Therefore, they need to be accompanied by policies that are able to adapt quickly to change and self-transform. Third, the major challenges are related to the emergence and involvement of new actors, public, private, individual (citizens), collective including foundations and associations. Taking these new actors into account should lead to new forms of agency behavior that are not centralized by governments, but distributed, by which we would distinguish in particular the role of social entrepreneurs (Battilana et al. 2009). The emergence of these new actors also questions the notions of legitimacy and responsibility. To what extent are they legitimate and accountable, and in what proportion vis-à-vis government or public decision-makers? Finally, from an economic point of view, addressing these major challenges should lead to a different, intelligent, inclusive and sustainable economic growth.

Given the above-mentioned specificities, avenues for reflection on the need to design and implement new forms of public innovation policies have emerged. According to Mazzucato (2018), public policymakers cannot face major challenges such as the energy transition by relying on the traditional concepts of externality and public goods. We need to go further, beyond the framework of economic analysis in terms of market failures, to a vision of co-creating and co-designing new markets (Mazzucato 2016). The analytical framework mobilized is that of mission-oriented policy, the term referring to public policy programs targeted at major societal challenges rates. "A range of existing mission-oriented R&D programs can provide useful guidance for the design of new programs aimed at these challenges" (Foray et al. 2012, p. 1697). For his part, Hekkert et al. (2020, p. 76) defines these missions as "an urgent strategic goal that requires transformative systems change directed toward overcoming a wicked societal problem". These forms of intervention can furthermore be brought closer to the issue of mobilizing demand-side policy instruments (Edler and Georghiou 2007; Edquist et al. 2015; Shot and Steinmueller 2018).

In the context of mission-oriented policies, governments have to play a more significant role than they usually do, for example by facilitating and orchestrating relevant initiatives of societal actors, and/or by creating spaces for innovation interactions. The aim is to influence not only the number of innovations but also their direction. Compared to earlier innovation policies with the State at the center, the pitfalls of highly top-down or bottom-up missions must be avoided (Mazzucato 2018). In this context, the use of digital tools – platforms, hubs, Big Data – or combinations of digital and non-digital tools, can facilitate the orchestration mission that the State should lead. Indeed, the use of digital tools allows a call to the crowd and more inclusiveness. These tools can be very useful to find a balance between state interventionism and citizen participation. It remains to be defined which tools or combination of tools will be the most appropriate to face each major challenge, and which mode of governance will have to be put in place.

These digital tools, and their ability to propose transversal forms that allow the State and stakeholders to interact, can also meet the needs of socially oriented innovation policies, such as the Responsible Research and Innovation (RRI) that Europe calls for (Pellé and Reber 2016; European Commission 2017; Maesschalck 2017). RRI is defined as "a transparent and interactive process by which social actors, researchers, and innovators collaborate for the ethical acceptability, sustainability, and societal relevance of innovation – thus enabling the insertion of scientific and technical advances into society" (Von Schomberg 2013). To this end, digital tools could contribute to this process by proposing original devices that facilitate the interactions between the various stakeholders at all stages of the innovation process: collecting opinions, evaluating ex post, making adjustments and corrections to the initial innovation project if necessary.

From citizen science to AI

The movement to transform public policy as a whole is underway, as we have seen previously. This transformation is still in its infancy. Other forces are at work, whose scope and implications are difficult to measure today. Two movements under construction can be identified: citizen science and AI.

Public actors, driven by a growing need to mobilize citizens' skills to support them in the definition, construction or implementation of public services, may be led to mobilize the citizen science mechanism. Citizen science reflects the ability of the citizen to get involved in science-oriented research programs (Strasser et al. 2018; Heigl et al. 2019). The general idea is that amateurs (the general public) can contribute to the production of scientific knowledge (e.g. data feedback from the field), with an underlying desire to also meet an educational objective. The forms are very varied and can fall into the five categories of citizen involvement around data (Strasser et al. 2018): capturing, calculating, analyzing, evaluating and doing. Citizen science fits into the broader concept of citizen sourcing, proposed in the introduction to this book.

This citizen science, which has been echoed in some recent reports from European and American organizations, is closely combined with crowdsourcing (Howe 2006) by which, thanks to a digital platform, an actor has recourse to the expertise of a crowd, a community or individuals to answer a question, a challenge or a piece of advice. Crowdsourcing has seen a marked interest in recent years, not only from the point of view of subjects but also from the point of view of the diversity of actors. On the one hand, the use of the crowd's expertise in a short time has led companies to use this channel to ask for any kind of advice, to benefit from votes to select a product, a logo and even to post innovation questions[1]. On the other hand, this bottom-up vision, coupled with the possibilities offered by digital platforms, has been well received in recent years by public actors who have seen it as a way to accelerate their research programs and benefit from the

---

1 www.innocentive.com.

information and knowledge of citizens. NASA, for example, has launched several citizen science projects allowing 1 million volunteers from around the world to collaborate with scientists, notably in the collection of data on biodiversity, the exploration of the sun, comets and planets outside the solar system (NASA 2020). Europe, for its part, within the framework of its H2020 program, demonstrated its desire to place the citizen at the heart of its action (science for and with the citizen).

The other movement at work is the growing importance of AI. Its implementation in digital platforms is the subject of increasing analysis and its deployment will not be without effect on the public sphere. From a general point of view, many studies are interested in the effects of AI, its role in corporate strategy and its consequences in terms of employment (Acquatella et al. 2020). Driven by machine learning and deep learning and fed by massive data (Big Data), AI is becoming an essential component for better understanding consumer behavior, for developing more targeted advertising campaigns, etc. Chatbots are an illustration of this, they can be at the heart of a quest to improve the user experience (Daumal 2015) – and this at all levels – in order to achieve a high level of personalization. As highlighted in the Conseil d'État report (2017):

> [...] the dynamic of individualization of service is also and above all the result of the growing sophistication of algorithms and the development of artificial intelligence. By allowing massive, precise and instantaneous use of the almost infinite amount of digital data that can be mobilized, whether intentionally delivered by the user or available in the "big data", the platforms allow each person to sort information, products or services, to prioritize them and to select them according to their own criteria and needs or sources of satisfaction, which can even be combined: quality-price ratio, environmental value of the product or service, social value (Conseil d'État 2017, p. 38).

AI relies on machine learning algorithms that memorize and then scrutinize via big data mining (LeCun et al. 2015). In this sense, the machine is becoming more and more powerful. In order to function, AI relies on machine learning technology interfaces. The interface uses algorithms to create automatic learning models weaving to process large volumes of data and generate predictions. These algorithms include deep learning (Laudau et al. 2016): automatic learning based on artificial neural networks inspired by the human brain. The algorithms learn via the extraction of massive data and by comparison. This ability of the algorithm to process massive data as well as to extract a dynamic understanding of it contributes to providing analyses that can be predictive or prescriptive.

If private platforms, whether transaction or innovation platforms, were the first to put AI at the heart of their strategy (Acquatella et al. 2020), platforms set up by public actors have also seized the opportunities offered by this technology. Chevalier (2018) does not hesitate to put forward the term platform-state, for which the use of these technologies (AI in particular) can help meet certain injunctions/demands of the citizen for improved services:

> The development of the State-platform leads to pose the question of public service in new terms. First of all, it is likely to produce better quality services, fed by the massive collection of data and the resources of artificial intelligence, and better adapted to the expectations of users, brought to assert their point of view concerning the content of the services offered: the idea of "co-production" of the public service, which a certain number of sociological studies had highlighted, thus acquires a new scope; involved in the delivery of services, the citizen would become "co-responsible and co-producer of public goods", which would help to restore confidence in public action. The use of the digital tool would make it possible to go beyond the principle of equality, to offer a personalized service, taking into account individual situations (Chevalier 2018, p. 10).

However, the consideration of new technologies, of which AI is a part, in the production or delivery of public services is not without difficulties for the public actor. Two major issues, highlighted by the report of the Conseil d'État (2017), are to be underlined. On the one hand, the introduction and use of these new technologies by the private sector may lead the latter to take a new look at services previously provided by the public sector, and to find a new form of profitability in them. The scope of public service is known to be evolving, but the arrival of these technologies has accelerated this trend. The Conseil d'État (2017) gives the example of Bison Futé, whose recent competition from Coyote or Waze has precipitated its fall:

> Because of the technical possibilities offered by digital technology, with very little investment and a particularly low operating cost, the economic model of the digital platform can make activities that were not previously profitable. And even though these activities could have been seen as public services by nature, this evolution can lead to their spontaneous takeover by private initiative (Conseil d'État 2017, p. 98)

On the other hand, new public service activities or the reinforcement of certain others may be the consequence of the arrival of AI. The applications in terms of data processing for health, defense, agronomy, weather, education, justice, transportation and mobility are an illustration (Charlet and Bringey 2010). At the same time, the public sector may be required to build new digital platforms in order to promote innovation around AI: this is the case, for example, with the French platform beta.gouv.fr, which identifies innovation issues (and AI in particular) and relies on a community of diverse actors (civil servants, external partners) to find solutions to these issues.

What about public policy evaluations in a digitalized environment?

The question of public policy evaluation has been addressed indirectly through the various contributions to the book, by focusing on the consequences of digitalization on the way public action is (re)designed. However, the various chapters suggest that digital tools also have direct consequences on the practice of evaluation itself. Without claiming to be exhaustive, we would like to mention here those that deserve an extension in future work.

Without going into the details of each of these approaches, it should be remembered that evaluation is a particularly complex subject in the French case. Although the notion of "scientific judgment of value" (Perret 2004) seems to be shared, there is no consensus on a definition within the community of "evaluators", unlike in English-speaking countries (Delahais et al. 2021). And for good reason, this community is in fact made up of actors with numerous and heterogeneous objectives: control and monitoring of government action and laws (Parliament), control of the use of public funds (Cour des comptes, inspections générales), production of public studies for information purposes (INSEE, France Stratégie) or to assist decision-making (ministerial statistical services), accountability (local authorities), production of scientific knowledge (researchers), maintenance or development of an economic activity (consulting firms, independent). These purposes are of course not exclusive, and each of the actors mentioned may pursue intersecting objectives (e.g. seeking accountability while pursuing the improvement of the policy or program being evaluated). Another element of complexity lies in the method used. For the same purpose, a political scientist will not use the same methodological corpus as an economist. Likewise, both will be able to mobilize the evaluation at different times: upstream of the implementation of public policy, during its implementation, at the end of its implementation. The digitalization movement described above, which allows for the development of ever more extensive databases and ever more efficient methods of analysis, could in a sense contribute to greater convergence within the community of evaluators by sharing a harmonized methodological approach to the question of data. Indeed, we might expect the various actors to integrate these data into their work on the basis of common foundations (with, of course, methodologies that are more or less segregated according to the means available and the purpose): identical tools and analysis language, results based on shared references to the recognized principles of the scientific method of data analysis, etc. The study of the development of the use of microsimulation tools seems to point in this direction. Initially used by economic researchers, these models have gradually spread to ministerial statistical services, central administrations, activist associations and more recently to Parliament. The evaluation of bills and proposals is simplified since, in some cases, results can be obtained in a few hours or days, compared to several weeks or even months, with other approaches; the evaluation of certain amendments by the parliamentarians themselves is thereby permitted; research organizations have more means of verifying by themselves the evaluations produced by the public authorities. From there to see a "revolution" in evaluative practice, there is only one step: "With the Leximpact interface [microsimulator of the Assemblée Nationale], we have for the first time this year a real simulation and evaluation tool for our amendments" (Jean-Noël Barrot deputy for Yvelines, discussion session on the 2020 finance bill, October 14, 2019).

However, the dissemination of evaluation tools exploiting the possibilities offered by digitalization also brings its share of complexity and limitations. First, there is the question of accessibility to these new tools. In addition to questions of intellectual property and the "openness" (most microsimulation models, for example, are now in Open Access), their use is far from being "push-button". Indeed, it implies knowledge and skills in terms of data analysis which, at the beginning of 2022, are not fully mastered in the same way by the members of the evaluation community. Only those trained in economics and statistics, or self-trained in the case of "data geeks", know how to use such tools and interpret their results.

It remains to be seen to what extent the gap is widening among evaluators, how deep it is and, above all, whether the evaluation of public policies can still ignore their exploitation in the age of mass data. This question is all the more central in that the possibilities of exploitation have not stopped developing. To take just one example, the Assemblée Nationale's model can now be mobilized for reform projects other than income tax reform, and is constantly being improved.

The corollary of this increase in the complexity of the method is the question of access to the resources necessary for such evaluations, and in particular to data. The various chapters have clearly shown the decisive nature of this access. Although not all actors have access to the same data depending on their status, we have noted that some do not have access to it because of a lack of knowledge of rights in this area. The precise reconstruction of the conditions of access and exploitation in this area is constantly evolving, and would deserve a more holistic and dedicated exploration than the present work.

Finally, despite the relative fantasy generated around the possibilities of using data and the resulting "revolutions" (the reality being most of the time very far from collective representations), it should be noted that the evaluations produced by means of digitalization data and the instruments thus produced retain a largely limited scope. On the one hand, the data is not always available (in particular at the level of local authorities), and their use is often not sufficient on its own to achieve the expected purposes mentioned above. On the other hand, the mere mobilization of these new instruments alone would not suffice to produce an evaluation, the interpretations resulting from the figures not being, for the time being, digitizable. The risk is then to settle for "simplistic" evaluations, and to forget the interpretative force consubstantial with any evaluation (the "evaluative judgment"), permitted by scientific approaches, but which have proven their worth.

References

Acquatella, F., Fernandez, V., Houy, T. (2020). Les stratégies de plateformes analysées sous le prisme de l'intelligence artificielle. *Question(s) de management*, 4(30), 63–76.

Battilana, J., Leca, B., Boxenbaum, E. (2009). How actors change institutions: Towards a theory of institutional entrepreneurship. *Academy of Management Annals*, 3(1), 65–107.

Cagnin, C., Amanatidou, E., Keenan, M. (2012). Orienting European innovation systems towards grand challenges and the roles that FTA can play. *Science and Public Policy*, 39(2), 140–152.

Charlet, J. and Bringay, S. (2019). Intelligence artificielle et Santé. Une analyse rétrospective depuis 2010. *30es Journées francophones d'ingénierie des connaissances*, IC, 26–42.

Conseil d'État (2017). Puissance publique et plateformes numériques : accompagner l'uberisation. Report, Conseil d'État, Paris.

Chevallier, J. (2018). Vers l'État-plateforme ? *Revue française d'administration publique*, 3(167), 627–637.

Commission Européenne (2017). Horizon 2020. Work Programme 2018–2020: Science with and for Society. Report, Decision, C(2017)7124.

Daumal, S. (2017). *Design d'expérience utilisateur : principes et méthodes UX.* Éditions Eyrolles, Paris.

Delahais, T., Devaux-Spatarakis, A., Revillard, A., Ridde, V. (2021). *Évaluation. Fondement, controverses, perspectives*. Édition Science et Bien Commun, Quebec.

Edler, J. and Georghiou, L. (2007). Public procurement and innovation – Resurrecting the demand side. *Research Policy*, 36(7), 949–963.

Edquist, C. and Zabala-Iturriagagoitia, J.M. (2015). Pre-commercial procurement: A demand or supply policy instrument in relation to innovation? *R&D Management*, 45(2), 147–160.

Foray, D., Mowery, D.C., Nelson, R.R. (2012). Public R&D; and social challenges: What lessons from mission R&D; Programs? *Research Policy*, 41(10), 1697–1702.

Heigl, F., Kieslinger, B., Paul, K.T., Uhlik, J., Dörler, D. (2019). Opinion: Toward an international definition of citizen science. *Proceedings of the National Academy of Sciences*, 116(17), 8089–8092.

Hekkert, M.P., Janssen, M.J., Wesseling, J.H., Negro, S.O. (2020). Mission-oriented innovation systems. *Environmental Innovation and Societal Transitions*, 34, 76–79.

Hicks, D. (2016). Grand challenges in US science policy attempt policy innovation. *International Journal of Foresight and Innovation Policy*, 11(1–3), 22–42.

Howes, J. (2006). The rise of crowdsourcing. *Wired Magazine*, 14(6).

Kaldewey, D. (2018). The grand challenges discourse: Transforming identity work in science and science policy. *Minerva*, 56(2), 161–182.

Kallerud, E., Amanatidou, E., Upham, P., Nieminen, M., Klitkou, A., Olsen, D.S., Scordato, L. (2013). Dimensions of research and innovation policies to address grand and global challenges. Report, WP 13, Manchester Business School.

Kuhlmann, S. and Rip, A. (2014). The challenge of addressing grand challenges. *report to the european research and innovation area board*.

Kuhlmann, S. and Rip, A. (2018). Next-generation innovation policy and grand challenges. *Science and Public Policy*, 45(4), 448–454.

Landau, I.D. and Landau, V. (2016), Data mining et machine learning dans les big data une tentative de demystification. *Conference – GIPSA –LAB*, Grenoble.

LeCun, Y., Bengio, Y. Hinton, G. (2015). Deep learning. *Nature*, 521(7553), 436–444.

Linders, D. (2012). From e-government to we-government: Defining a typology for citizen coproduction in the age of social media. *Government Information Quarterly*, 29(4), 446–454.

Lindner, R., Daimer, S., Beckert, B., Heyen, N., Koehler, J., Teufel, B., Wydra, S. (2016). Addressing directionality: Orientation failure and the systems of innovation heuristic. Towards reflexive governance. *Fraunhofer ISI Discussion Papers – Innovation Systems and Policy Analysis*, 52.

Lukesch, R., Ludvig, A., Slee, B., Weiss, G., Živojinović, I. (2020). Social innovation, societal change, and the role of policies. *Sustainability*, 12(18), 7407.

Maesschalck, M. (2017). *Reflexive Governance for Research and Innovative Knowledge*. ISTE Ltd, London and John Wiley & Sons, New York.

Mazzucato, M. (2016). From market fixing to market-creating: A new framework for innovation policy. *Industry and Innovation*, 23(2), 140–156.

Mazzucato, M. (2018). Mission-oriented research & innovation in the European Union. Report, European Commission.

NASA (2020). Open innovation at NASA: Enhancing problem solving and discovery through prize competitions, challenges, crowdsourcing, and citizen sourcing [Online]. Available at: https://www.nasa.gov/sites/default/files/atoms/files/2019_nasa_open_innovation_report_final.pdf.

Pellé, S. and Reber, B. (2016). *From Ethical Review to Responsible Research and Innovation*. ISTE Ltd, London, & John Wiley & Sons, Hoboken.

Perret, B. (2014). *L'évaluation des politiques publiques*. La Découverte, Paris.

Schot, J. and Steinmueller, W.E. (2018). Three frames for innovation policy: R&D, systems of innovation and transformative change. *Research Policy*, 47(9), 1554–1567.

Strasser, B., Baudry, J., Mahr, D., Sanchez, G., Tancoigne, E. (2019). Citizen science? Rethinking science and public participation. *Science & Technology Studies*, 32(2), 52–76.

Ulnicane, I. (2016). "Grand challenges" concept: A return of the "big ideas" in science, technology and innovation policy? *International Journal of Foresight and Innovation Policy*, 11(1–3), 5–21.

Van der Have, R.P. and Rubalcaba, L. (2016). Social innovation research: An emerging area of innovation studies? *Research Policy*, 45(9), 1923–1935.

Von Schomberg, R. (2013). A vision of responsible research and innovation. In *Responsible Innovation*, Owen, R., Heintz, M., Bessant, J. (eds). Wiley, London.

List of Authors

Franck BESSIS
Triangle
Université Lumière Lyon 2
France

Paul COTTON
Triangle
Sciences Po Lyon
France

Claudine GAY
Triangle
Université Lumière Lyon 2
France

Isabelle LIOTARD
CEPN
Université Sorbonne Paris Nord
Villetaneuse
France

Valérie REVEST
Magellan
Université Jean Moulin Lyon 3
iaelyon School of Management
France

Audrey VÉZIAN
Triangle, CNRS
Lyon
France

Index

Other titles from

in

Information Systems, Web and Pervasive Computing

2022

ACCART Jean-Philippe
Library Transformation Strategies

BOADA Martí, LAZARO Antonio, GIRBAU David, VILLARINO Ramón
Battery-less NFC Sensors for the Internet of Things

BRÉZILLON Patrick, TURNER Roy M.
Modeling and Use of Context in Action

CHAMOUX Jean-Pierre
The Digital Era 3: Customs and Practices

KARAM Elie
General Contractor Business Model for Smart Cities: Fundamentals and Techniques

2021

BEN REBAH Hassen, BOUKTHIR Hafedh, CHÉDEBOIS Antoine
Website Design and Development with HTML5 and CSS3

EL ASSAD Safwan, BARBA Dominique
Digital Communications 1: Fundamentals and Techniques
Digital Communications 2: Directed and Practical Work

GAUDIN Thierry, MAUREL Marie-Christine, POMEROL Jean-Charles
Chance, Calculation and Life

LAURENT Sébastien-Yves
Conflicts, Crimes and Regulations in Cyberspace
(Cybersecurity Set – Volume 2)

LE DEUFF Olivier
Hyperdocumentation (Intellectual Technologies Set – Volume 9)

PÉLISSIER Maud
Cultural Commons in the Digital Ecosystem
(Intellectual Technologies Set – Volume 8)

2020

CLIQUET Gérard, with the collaboration of BARAY Jérôme
Location-Based Marketing: Geomarketing and Geolocation

DE FRÉMINVILLE Marie
Cybersecurity and Decision Makers: Data Security and Digital Trust

GEORGE Éric
Digitalization of Society and Socio-political Issues 2: Digital, Information and Research

HELALI Saida
Systems and Network Infrastructure Integration

LOISEAU Hugo, VENTRE Daniel, ADEN Hartmut
Cybersecurity in Humanities and Social Sciences: A Research Methods Approach (Cybersecurity Set – Volume 1)

SEDKAOUI Soraya, KHELFAOUI Mounia
Sharing Economy and Big Data Analytics

SCHMITT Églantine
Big Data: An Art of Decision Making
(Intellectual Technologies Set – Volume 7)

2019

ALBAN Daniel, EYNAUD Philippe, MALAURENT Julien, RICHET Jean-Loup, VITARI Claudio
Information Systems Management: Governance, Urbanization and Alignment

AUGEY Dominique, with the collaboration of ALCARAZ Marina
Digital Information Ecosystems: Smart Press

BATTON-HUBERT Mireille, DESJARDIN Eric, PINET François
Geographic Data Imperfection 1: From Theory to Applications

BRIQUET-DUHAZÉ Sophie, TURCOTTE Catherine
From Reading-Writing Research to Practice

BROCHARD Luigi, KAMATH Vinod, CORBALAN Julita, HOLLAND Scott, MITTELBACH Walter, OTT Michael
Energy-Efficient Computing and Data Centers

CHAMOUX Jean-Pierre
The Digital Era 2: Political Economy Revisited

COCHARD Gérard-Michel
Introduction to Stochastic Processes and Simulation

DUONG Véronique
SEO Management: Methods and Techniques to Achieve Success

GAUCHEREL Cédric, GOUYON Pierre-Henri, DESSALLES Jean-Louis
Information, The Hidden Side of Life

GEORGE Éric
Digitalization of Society and Socio-political Issues 1: Digital, Communication and Culture

GHLALA Riadh
Analytic SQL in SQL Server 2014/2016

JANIER Mathilde, SAINT-DIZIER Patrick
Argument Mining: Linguistic Foundations

SOURIS Marc
Epidemiology and Geography: Principles, Methods and Tools of Spatial Analysis

TOUNSI Wiem
Cyber-Vigilance and Digital Trust: Cyber Security in the Era of Cloud Computing and IoT

2018

ARDUIN Pierre-Emmanuel
Insider Threats
(Advances in Information Systems Set – Volume 10)

CARMÈS Maryse
Digital Organizations Manufacturing: Scripts, Performativity and Semiopolitics
(Intellectual Technologies Set – Volume 5)

CARRÉ Dominique, VIDAL Geneviève
Hyperconnectivity: Economical, Social and Environmental Challenges
(Computing and Connected Society Set – Volume 3)

CHAMOUX Jean-Pierre
The Digital Era 1: Big Data Stakes

DOUAY Nicolas
Urban Planning in the Digital Age
(Intellectual Technologies Set – Volume 6)

FABRE Renaud, BENSOUSSAN Alain
The Digital Factory for Knowledge: Production and Validation of Scientific Results

GAUDIN Thierry, LACROIX Dominique, MAUREL Marie-Christine, POMEROL Jean-Charles
Life Sciences, Information Sciences

GAYARD Laurent
Darknet: Geopolitics and Uses
(Computing and Connected Society Set – Volume 2)

IAFRATE Fernando
Artificial Intelligence and Big Data: The Birth of a New Intelligence
(Advances in Information Systems Set – Volume 8)

LE DEUFF Olivier
Digital Humanities: History and Development
(Intellectual Technologies Set – Volume 4)

MANDRAN Nadine
Traceable Human Experiment Design Research: Theoretical Model and
Practical Guide
(Advances in Information Systems Set – Volume 9)

PIVERT Olivier
NoSQL Data Models: Trends and Challenges

ROCHET Claude
Smart Cities: Reality or Fiction

SALEH Imad, AMMI, Mehdi, SZONIECKY Samuel
Challenges of the Internet of Things: Technology, Use, Ethics
(Digital Tools and Uses Set – Volume 7)

SAUVAGNARGUES Sophie
Decision-making in Crisis Situations: Research and Innovation for Optimal
Training

SEDKAOUI Soraya
Data Analytics and Big Data

SZONIECKY Samuel
Ecosystems Knowledge: Modeling and Analysis Method for Information and
Communication
(Digital Tools and Uses Set – Volume 6)

2017

BOUHAÏ Nasreddine, SALEH Imad
Internet of Things: Evolutions and Innovations
(Digital Tools and Uses Set – Volume 4)

DUONG Véronique
Baidu SEO: Challenges and Intricacies of Marketing in China

LESAS Anne-Marie, MIRANDA Serge
The Art and Science of NFC Programming
(Intellectual Technologies Set – Volume 3)

LIEM André
Prospective Ergonomics
(Human-Machine Interaction Set – Volume 4)

MARSAULT Xavier
Eco-generative Design for Early Stages of Architecture
(Architecture and Computer Science Set – Volume 1)

REYES-GARCIA Everardo
The Image-Interface: Graphical Supports for Visual Information
(Digital Tools and Uses Set – Volume 3)

REYES-GARCIA Everardo, BOUHAÏ Nasreddine
Designing Interactive Hypermedia Systems
(Digital Tools and Uses Set – Volume 2)

SAÏD Karim, BAHRI KORBI Fadia
Asymmetric Alliances and Information Systems:Issues and Prospects
(Advances in Information Systems Set – Volume 7)

SZONIECKY Samuel, BOUHAÏ Nasreddine
Collective Intelligence and Digital Archives: Towards Knowledge
Ecosystems
(Digital Tools and Uses Set – Volume 1)

2016

BEN CHOUIKHA Mona
Organizational Design for Knowledge Management

BERTOLO David
Interactions on Digital Tablets in the Context of 3D Geometry Learning
(Human-Machine Interaction Set – Volume 2)

BOUVARD Patricia, SUZANNE Hervé
Collective Intelligence Development in Business

EL FALLAH SEGHROUCHNI Amal, ISHIKAWA Fuyuki, HÉRAULT Laurent, TOKUDA Hideyuki
Enablers for Smart Cities

FABRE Renaud, in collaboration with MESSERSCHMIDT-MARIET Quentin, HOLVOET Margot
New Challenges for Knowledge

GAUDIELLO Ilaria, ZIBETTI Elisabetta
Learning Robotics, with Robotics, by Robotics
(Human-Machine Interaction Set – Volume 3)

HENROTIN Joseph
The Art of War in the Network Age
(Intellectual Technologies Set – Volume 1)

KITAJIMA Munéo
Memory and Action Selection in Human–Machine Interaction
(Human–Machine Interaction Set – Volume 1)

LAGRAÑA Fernando
E-mail and Behavioral Changes: Uses and Misuses of Electronic Communications

LEIGNEL Jean-Louis, UNGARO Thierry, STAAR Adrien
Digital Transformation
(Advances in Information Systems Set – Volume 6)

NOYER Jean-Max
Transformation of Collective Intelligences
(Intellectual Technologies Set – Volume 2)

VENTRE Daniel
Information Warfare – 2nd edition

VITALIS André
The Uncertain Digital Revolution
(Computing and Connected Society Set – Volume 1)

2011

BANOS Arnaud, THÉVENIN Thomas
Geographical Information and Urban Transport Systems

DAUPHINÉ André
Fractal Geography

LEMBERGER Pirmin, MOREL Mederic
Managing Complexity of Information Systems

STOCKINGER Peter
Introduction to Audiovisual Archives

STOCKINGER Peter
Digital Audiovisual Archives

VENTRE Daniel
Cyberwar and Information Warfare

2010

BONNET Pierre
Enterprise Data Governance

BRUNET Roger
Sustainable Geography

CARREGA Pierre
Geographical Information and Climatology

CAUVIN Colette, ESCOBAR Francisco, SERRADJ Aziz
Thematic Cartography – 3-volume series
Thematic Cartography and Transformations – Volume 1
Cartography and the Impact of the Quantitative Revolution – Volume 2
New Approaches in Thematic Cartography – Volume 3

LANGLOIS Patrice
Simulation of Complex Systems in GIS

MATHIS Philippe
Graphs and Networks – 2ⁿᵈ edition

Printed and bound by CPI Group (UK) Ltd, Croydon, CR0 4YY

27/10/2024

14580734-0001